QUIET THE NOISE

Rami F. Odeh, MS

QUIET THE NOISE

A Trail Runner's Path to Hearing God

Published in the United States of America

EAN-13- 9781545061374
Biography & Autobiography / Personal Memoirs
13.08.29

DEDICATION

This book is first and foremost dedicated to our Lord, Jesus Christ, without whom nothing is possible. It is also dedicated to my wonderful family—Heather, Ryan and Hana—and to all the people out there who have a tough time "quieting their minds" long enough to hear our Lord!

Why Write This Book?
How did I do it?

All of my adult life I have wanted to write a book. I would imagine almost everyone has had this desire at some point in their lives. Sometimes, while spending hours in a book store, I think that everyone has written some type of book, except me, since there are so many titles! In 2008 I started an on-line blog to chronicle my runs and path to the Lord. After some positive comments and a few; "you should really write a book", I started seriously thinking about starting this project, even going to the extreme of putting "Work on Book" on my to do list, but to no avail. Really nothing got started 'till one fateful today in May 2009 when the president of a local college asked me if I would be interested in teaching a new course they were offering in Sports Psychology. That night at dinner, when I told my family I might be taking on a 3rd job (running our fitness business, working part time at a local hospital and now teaching a class) my 7 year old son, Ryan, reminded me, "Dad, you will now have *four* jobs: don't forget the book you are writing". Amazing, from the mouths of babes. So, I promised him I would start that day and put his name in the dedication.

Fast forward two months, with no progress on the book. Seeing me on computer when he comes downstairs to say goodnight, Ryan says, "Just checking Dad—how is that book going?" and "I want to see how far you have gotten" and "I cannot wait to have the party when it is done and see it and tell all my friends my dad is an *author*!" OK, I am listening to you and getting it done!

Fast forward another two months. Amazing…now I am getting messages from my 4-year-old daughter, Hana! Hana and I have a "date" while my wife, Heather, and Ryan go to a birthday party. We rent a movie and cuddle on the couch and enjoy each other's company. At the end she looks at me sort of quizzically and starts a conversation about my work habits. It goes something like this:

"Daddy, I don't want you to work anymore. You work too much." I work about 50 hours per week, which, comparatively, is not a lot, especially because I never travel, but I don't argue! "Why don't you want me to work?" I ask.

"Because I want to spend every day with you". At this point, I am ready to sell the company and become Mr. Mom, such a precious moment! A teachable moment, an opportunity which I decide to take. "Hana, do you know why Daddy works?"

"No," she answers thoughtfully.

"Daddy works because, first of all, he loves his job. He also works to provide money so we can have a home, food to eat, your school, our clothes, etc."

She thinks about this for a bit and says, "I have an idea, let's just use my allowance for money." Here is another opportunity.

"Do you know how you get your allowance?"

"No."

"From Daddy working." She's thinking about that.

But then she tries another tactic: "Just tell the people you work for that you want to work less, maybe 2 days per week". Now, this is one smart girl—she knows we own our own business.

So, my response is, "Hana, do you know who daddy works for."

"No".

"Daddy is daddy's boss." That should do it. But she just pauses a moment and solves the problem for both of us:

"Well, then it is easy to work less!" I know when to quit—she's got me, fair and square. I decided at that moment to spend more quality time with them, more time pursuing my gift of the Holy Spirit (this book, presenting and promoting my passion)—The commitment, to write at least 60 minutes one day a week, was made that day! 3 years after that day....

CONTENTS

PART ONE

Chapter 1: The early years...17
    Riding Motocross 17
    Running in gym class......................................19
    Run to ride...20
    Run to win..21

Chapter 2: A year of big changes 23
    Career change 23
    Death in the family..25

Chapter 3: Getting started..27
    The First Triathlon, March 1992.....................27
    The First Marathon, Spring 1993...................29

Chapter 4: Nowhere to be...31
    Tour of Italy, Dolomites, June 1997 31
    Ironman Florida, 1999 33

Riding the mountains 39
Deer Moments.. 39

Chapter 5: Something new **41**
I need a break.. 41
Hiking, Fall 2007 42
The first trail races, Spring 2008................................. 43
Confirmation, 2008... 44

Chapter 6: The trail less traveled **47**
Daddy time 47
Race Day.. 49

PART TWO

Chapter 7: First Ultra, Mountain Mist 2009 ....**53**
Training 53
Race Day.. 55
The going gets tough... 56
AKA: Goat Boy 58

Chapter 8: Thankfulness..**61**
Planning Ultra 2 61
Race day... 63
Trouble... 65

Chapter 9: An unplanned day "off" **69**
That sinking feeling.. 69
Give it my best... 71

Chapter 10: Silence, Solitude and Suffering...................73

Broken promise... 73

Silence... 75

Suffering 75

Solitude... 76

Chapter 11: The 50 mile decision 103

100,000 steps 103

Time for "real" training 105

Easy, outdoor exercise 106

Chapter 12: Changes..109

The Stranger... 109

Silver lining.. 111

Embracing R & R.. 114

Chapter 13: Letting Go...115

Training the will 115

Christmas gift 117

Letting go, again 118

"Snow Jam 2011".. 119

Heather's workout... 120

Seeing God in action with others.............................. 121

Chapter 14: Training for 50 miler 125

Seven weeks to go 125

Night running... 127

9 Days to Go!.. 129

Chapter 15: The "Final" Chapter 131

   Training program summary 131

   Race day prep 132

   First lap 135

   Round two 138

   Final loop 140

   Lessons from the journey 143

Chapter 16: What's next? 145

   100 miles? 145

   Running with others 147

   Avoidance 149

   Change of plans 151

   4 miles of bliss 152

Epilogue: Running and forgiveness 155

Appendix: Setting goals 159

   Poorly defined goals 159

   Unrealistic goals 160

   Failure to accept limitations 160

   Lack of commitment 161

PART ONE

The sufferings of the present moment are not worthy to be compared to the glory that is to come.

Romans 8:18

CHAPTER 1

THE EARLY YEARS

Athletes work hard to win a crown that cannot last, but we do it for a crown that will last forever. I don't run without a goal.

1 Corinthians 9:24-27

Riding Motocross

I first realized you could connect to God through sports and movement during my first year of racing motocross (off-road dirt bike racing). The first time I ever got on a (borrowed!) motorcycle at age ten, I neglected to mention to the owner of the bike that I had no idea how to ride—rushing into new things without preparation is a common theme in my life—and I proceeded to crash into a brick wall. This should have been a warning, but I am very, very stubborn so, naturally, I went on to get my first off-road motorcycle, a Suzuki "Trailhopper" 50cc, the next year when I was eleven. Most of my friends had off-road motorcycles and just about all of them had begun racing them by the time we were all thirteen.

In the fall of 1976, I began my fourteen-year motocross "career" at South Woods MX track in Cairo, NY, riding a bike that my half-brother, Mike, helped me buy and sneak into my garage. All my buddies were racing, so I wanted to try it.

Of course, it was cold and raining like crazy when we lined up for practice at a track about three hours from my house. Since practice started at 9 am, we had to get up at 5 am on a Sunday to get there on time—a theme that has persisted in all the sports I have actively participated in throughout my adult life!

I can remember it like it was yesterday, waiting in a small, overcrowded corral with three of my best friends (John "D", John "B" and Rick "D") to be let out for practice.

I had never been so nervous in my life. We were sitting in a crowded corral waiting for our turn to take a few practice laps in the mud and I was so scared I could not even breathe or see straight. Looking back I really wish I had been raised with some sort of organized religion or at least prayer life—an "Our Father" or "Hail Mary" really could have calmed me down.

When it came time to take off, my mind was racing and I really didn't even know where I was—I rode so badly that I forgot how to shift and I couldn't even make it one lap around without getting stuck in the mud! My goggles were fogged up, and I was in the strangest state. This was my first experience with the immense physical changes (and thus mental changes) that occur with exercise, especially in a heightened state.

I didn't even race that first day. It was so tough to get around the track most of us went home. Next time, at South Woods Motocross Park, in Monticello, NY, I managed to finish both motos (races), even though I was once again so nervous I could hardly remember how I did it. I continued to love this intense sport for many years.

The first of many experiences of connecting to God during intense physical exertion came many races later. I have always, always been a very anxious person. Preparing for these races was a big deal for me—I would check and double-check my equipment and make other preparations the day before and then still get up early on race day to check once again. I would be nervous all morning, fidgeting, expending way too much energy—but then something would happen as soon as I got my bike started on the line. A calmness would come over me: I was in the moment, focused, happy, excited, and thinking about nothing but the task at hand (quite a feat for me). This was my first introduction to what intense sports can do to calm the noisy mind and allow the Holy Spirit to enter in.

Running in gym class

In gym class we had to run around the track four times. I hated every minute of it. I was not last but I wasn't first, either. There were guys who finished a good 2-3 minutes ahead of me and actually seemed to enjoy this craziness! There had to be something seriously wrong with these people. I was in pain the whole time, never catching my breath, feeling like it would never be over. No peace of mind after it was done, probably because I couldn't stop thinking about having to do it again the week after. The only positive—a lesson in "don't quit something after the first time you do it." If I hadn't been willing to try running again—distance running, though, instead of sprints—I would never have discovered the joy of trail running.

Run to ride

At age fifteen, I had accumulated enough "win, place and show" points to move up to Expert class in motocross competition. The Expert class races were longer and more demanding. A 20-25 minute race might not seem like a long time, but anyone who has ridden a dirt bike will tell you that riding for 25 minutes is as demanding on the body as a total-body sprint for the whole time!

I decided I needed to get in better shape so I figured running would do it. My first run was not a huge accomplishment—I ran the half-mile around my block in my jeans and white Nike high tops, dying the whole time. For the sake of the sport I loved, I decided to keep doing a sport I hated. I even decided (here stubbornness was my friend!) I would just keep working at it until I got better. A runner was born.

Run to win

After I had been running for a few years, I did (surprise!) get better. And (bonus!), I found I didn't hate it like I had in school. In fact, I decided to sign up for a road race to see what they were like. I picked the Lake Mahopac, NY 10k and did some sporadic training for it. All I remember from this race was how much *harder* it was running in an organized competition than running on my own. I also realized that I was once again having that same in-the-moment, close-to-God experience I had often had when racing in motocross competitions.

It was a very hilly course. I was so busy trying to keep up with or pass people that I didn't keep track of the distance I had run or my speed. Even so, I ended up finishing in about 46-47 minutes, only 4 minutes off the fastest 10k I would later run at age 30 with the benefit of multiple races and tons of training.

Lesson here: while training is definitely a must, I feel that a very large percentage of athletic ability is a combination of genes and the power of the mind! I realized early on I didn't have the genetic make-up to be a great runner, but I do have a lot of drive and push myself to utilize every ounce of natural ability I do have and that determination (stubbornness!) goes a long way! Though I didn't realize it then, making the most of your resources is a basic Catholic principle. I was pleasing God without even knowing it!

As I am sure you can tell at this point in your reading, this book is NOT written by an elite runner! I am your average, middle of the pack runner who just happened to find out other reasons for running once he got off road and hit the trails…more on this later!

CHAPTER 2

A YEAR OF BIG CHANGES

I can do all things through Christ which strengtheneth me.

Philippians 4:13

Career change

Living life is like running a marathon. Life can go on a long time with nothing really major happening (good or bad or both) and then multiple major things happen in a very short span of time (if you have run a long distance running race you know this happens, multiple times, in almost every race)! Then things settle down for a while and the pattern repeats. This just might be God's way of challenging us and helping us grow and then giving us the time to learn and apply the lessons he has given us.

1992 was one of those years for me. In the beginning of that year, I started to have serious misgivings about the corporate career path I was on. After finishing an MS degree in Industrial/Organizational Psychology in 1988, I had taken a job at a medium sized credit card processing company where I helped to start a training and development department.

I had never worked full time in a corporation, never developed a training manual and never, ever, taught anything in my life—talk about a steep learning curve. The job was pretty cool for a while, growing the department, doing some fun travel (yes, travel is fun when you are 26 and single), and learning a lot about corporate America. Then I was offered a job to be a manager of a new department to help build sales. Again, no sales experience at all and it was a telemarketing department—cold calling and managing people who like to cold call.

One day I am in another 10 hour meeting and we are waiting around for the executive team to show up. The conversation starts about "if you had to do your life over, what would you do." It goes around the room and I cannot believe what I am hearing—these supposedly successful individuals would have done something very different with their lives (landscaper, painter, writer, etc.) than what they are doing. When the conversation came to me, I didn't even open my mouth and three people in the room said, "He would have done something in the exercise field." Obviously I was in the wrong place! I went home that night and started applying to graduate schools for a degree in Exercise Science. I was single and had no ties: I could "do my life over" after only 3.5 years in an unfulfilling corporate job! I was always the guy who would go ride his bike or run after work instead of going to happy hour, so this was a pretty logical move for me!

The first big change in 1992 was leaving corporate America and going back to school to get my degree in Exercise Physiology and starting a new career as a Personal Fitness Trainer.

Death in the family

I had just made my decision to go to graduate school when I had the worst day of my life. On May 1st, 1992, my mother called me and asked, "have you seen your father? – he never came home last night." I had no idea what she was talking about or where he might be. I spent the day trying to find him, calling his friends and family in NY and the Middle East, but no one had seen or heard from him. This was unlike him and I started to worry. When he didn't show up the next day I booked a flight for May 3rd and flew home.

When I landed I called my mom and a woman whom I didn't know answered the phone and said, "get home right away" and would not put my mom on the phone. I hardly spoke to my best friend who picked me up at the airport—looking back I think I knew the truth on May 1st but stayed in denial until I got the actual news. When I pulled into the driveway, my mom came out and uttered the words no son ever wants to hear, especially without any warning: "They found your father's body in the Croton Reservoir this morning; he drowned." She would not talk about what happened, and to this day disputes the police and coroner's report, no one really knows what happened to him and how he ended up drowning.

I had never before and have never since felt like I did in that moment, falling down in my driveway crying, unable to move. My friend Joey "D" carried me into the house and the rest of the day is a complete blur. Joey was amazing this day and many days afterwards, calling people and letting them know when I could not—a great friend who remains my friend to this day. Let's add to this situation: during my last conversation with my father he had been complaining about wanting to retire but not knowing how to do it, so I was frustrated with him and in a rush told him to "be a man and just make a decision." When he responded, "it sounds like you are disappointed in me," I said, "I am disappointed because I want you to be a man and stop complaining and decide what to do with your life". That is how the conversation ended and those are the last words I spoke to the man I loved more than anyone on this earth.

To this day, when the conversations come up about wishes and regrets, mine is to take that whole conversation back.

My mother did not handle his death well – she was very angry. No one was allowed in the house to pay their respects. We didn't even have a funeral or formal burial. After about a year, I convinced her to buy a cemetery plot and buried his ashes there, without ceremony. She and I and the caretaker were the only ones there. For years after, when I attended funerals I would cry for the loss of my dad and the loss of the opportunity to grieve for him.

So, in summary, in 1992; I lost my father, left the corporate world, went back to graduate school, moved to Miami, *and* lived through Hurricane Andrew that destroyed my brother's homes and business. Quite the year.

CHAPTER 3

GETTING STARTED

Don't you realize that your body is the temple of the
Holy Spirit, who lives in you and was given to you by
God? You do not belong to yourself.

1 Corinthians 6:19

The First Triathlon, March 1992

I seem to be a person that thrives on doing things that he
is not comfortable with. The first time I rode a motorcycle,
I was so nervous that I had no idea what I was doing. I got
my first corporate job in an area I had never trained in, and I
would soon by starting on a new sport that seemed way out
of my league.

In 1988 I went to watch a triathlon (swim, bike, run) in
Florida that a good friend (Tim "K") was doing: a mile swim
in the ocean, a 25 mile bike ride and a 10k run. I could not
imagine ever doing such a thing—these people were nuts!

Four years later, after doing a serious amount of bike riding (including a mistake where I did a 100 miles on a mountain bike, on the road, when I had signed up for a 62.5 mile ride – fun!), I decided I wanted to do a sprint triathlon (1/4 mile swim, 10 mile bike, 5k run). The running and biking would be easy, but I could not swim even one length of the pool!

I got swim lessons and trained on my own until I could swim for 15 minutes without stopping. Once I felt ready, I signed up for a tri that was about 200 miles from my house (didn't want anyone I knew to see me compete) and drove up the night before to stay in a hotel. I am having dinner the night before and I hear people talking about the water temperature (North Florida, in March, is actually pretty cool) and what wetsuits they were going to wear. Wetsuits? Aren't they for surfers?

So, race morning it is about 40 degrees out and the water temperature is 62. That might not sound cold to you, but it was. Someone tells me that if I don't have a wetsuit, I shouldn't get into the water until the start so I don't get hypothermic. I listen. Gun goes off, I jump in the water and *Blam – it is so freakin' cold I jump right back out*! I am standing next to the only other idiot without a wetsuit as everyone else swims merrily away from us. I try again, but it is so cold it takes my breath away every time I try to swim.

I adopted a "walking along the ground while pretending to do the breast stroke" so I could keep my head above water (I was worried about getting disqualified if I wasn't actually swimming). It took me over 15 minutes to "swim" a quarter mile. I was so cold I had to put on a sweatshirt to do the bike ride. Anyone who has done a triathlon will tell you how fun it is to try to put dry clothes on a wet body, especially when you cannot feel your fingers. The rest of the race was uneventful and I finished feeling great. Basically, I was hooked.

My next race was in South Florida and I figured nothing could get much worse. Nope, we had one of those rare morning rain storms which caused the waves to bump up to about 5-7 feet. I was getting spun around and knocked over. Must have swallowed about three gallons of water in that quarter mile (at least the water was warm). You would think I would have gotten the point and quit the sport at this point but what I realized is I never, ever feel more alive than when I am suffering and scared and triathlons didn't cease giving that feeling to me for the next 15 years! There's just something about doing intense physical challenges that makes you feel alive and in the moment.

I suppose this new sport really worked for me, over the next 15 years I competed in over 150 Multi-Sport events (racing almost every weekend for the first few years)!

The First Marathon, Spring 1993

I decided to sign up for my first marathon in 1992. No one I knew at the time was training for this distance, so I did 100% of the training on my own. At the time I was really focused on time, pacing, etc., and did not really get any spiritual insights or lessons from the experience. However,

I did get to experience the famous "wall" for the first time. At mile 20 I was running strong, talking to people, laughing, and comfortably running an 8:45 pace. At mile 22 I felt terrible and had trouble holding a 10 minute pace! A cup of Coke, a couple of bites of a chocolate bar, and all back to normal. 3:48 for my first marathon—not a bad time—left me wanting more!

CHAPTER 4

NOWHERE TO BE

When you walk, your steps will not be hampered;
when you run, you will not stumble.

Proverbs 4:12

Tour of Italy, Dolomites, June 1997

From 1992 to 1997, I probably averaged 15 multi-sport events and 10 running races per year (basically racing every other weekend). Looking back, I had quit the "party lifestyle" in 1988 and these competitions probably replaced the stimulation those parties brought to the addictive center in my brain that needs this type of stimulation.

I was also searching for meaning in my life and did not have any type of prayer or worship life and the racing and training was what I thought I needed to make me feel whole, connected, and peaceful. A good buddy invited me to do a cycling tour in Italy in the summer of 1997, and I jumped at the chance. What a wonderful experience. The scenery, the mountains, the wonderful food and drink, and being with 30 people all on the same "path" in life was very cool.

What I remember most about the trip, however, was the pace of life I enjoyed for 10 days. The comment we repeated daily was, "We have nowhere to be and all day to get there." How often does that happen in our hectic lives? I shut down all communication to the US and my life here and actually had the time (after riding 3-6 hours per day) to re-read "Atlas Shrugged" by Ayn Rand.

This might have really been the beginning of my connection of exercise and quiet time, and, thus, the connection to the Holy Spirit. I remember one day like it was yesterday, and one moment in particular. We were climbing the Passo de Stelvio (a mountain pass used in the Giro de Italia, one of the three major Grand Tours in cycling), the third highest paved road in Europe, usually closed to traffic due to snow. It was about 30k of climbing (18miles), so steep that at the bottom it was 75 degrees and at the top it was snowing and people were skiing, in June!

Because of the severity of the climb, we all separated pretty early and were mostly climbing alone (my favorite thing to do on a bike) and I remember one moment of being completely alone on a stretch of road with three feet of snow to my right. It was so quiet all I could hear was my bike, my breathing, and the sound of the snow dropping in clumps as it melted on the road.

I felt so alive, so perfect, and so peaceful—looking back I just wish I had had the connection to the Lord I have now to pray and say "thank you" for the moment and the beauty he provides (I am saying a prayer of thanks right now as I write this, 14 years later). We all have these moments, every day— we just need to SLOW DOWN to hear and appreciate them!

We all finished the climb and waited at the top for the whole group to finish. The last person up was a previous Olympic cyclist's dad, about 75 years old, who had been diagnosed with cancer and given 6 months to live about 8 years before this moment. Talk about a life-affirming moment—he had never finished this climb before and we all cheered him in. I think he died in the next year, so I am so glad I was there to witness that moment with him. I have goose bumps right now just writing about it.

Ironman Florida, 1999

Below you will see the write up I did after completing my first and only Ironman triathlon in 1999. I am purposely not changing the write up or format at all to show you how much my focus for doing these long events changed in the next 10 years. This thing reads like an accounting spreadsheet or computer flow chart!

3:30am: Alarm goes off, sleep was very sporadic, tough time falling asleep, a bit nervous. Up immediately and start to make breakfast:

1. 5 servings of oatmeal (a "bucket")
2. 4 whole eggs
3. PB and J sandwich
4. Watermelon

4:30am–very, very full! Only water from here till race start!

5:30am–down to transition, drop off bags, prep for race, feeling really good, very relaxed and prepared, very excited about the day, great weather, great course, very happy and blessed to be here

6:30am–walk down to swim start, CAN'T BELIEVE IT, I FORGOT HEART RATE MONITOR!, head back to bags, no way to get it, decide that is has happened for a reason and just "go with the day as it comes–still very relaxed".

7am: Swim–Start out very, very slow, not as crowded as I thought it would be, very calm water, feeling good, almost too easy, probably going too slow, but that is ok. Run into a few jellyfish, that gets my heart rate up! First lap, look at my watch, 36 minutes! Fastest I have ever swam and I am not tired at all. Second lap uneventful, much more peaceful, smooth and easy. AMAZINGLY, I DON'T WANT THE SWIM TO BE OVER! I am in really good shape.

8:15am:Transition #1–FRANTIC! out of the water in 1:14 something (yea, already ahead of schedule!), running up the beach, someone throws you down, pulls off your wetsuit, finally see Heather, I'm very happy and (again) feeling lucky to be doing this and feeling so good. Transition tent very crowded, hectic, takes me a long time to change and get out on the bike (had a lot of clothes and food I didn't need in my bag).

8:30am: Bike: Again, out on the bike, feeling sooooo good, trying to hold back, 20mph feels like my heart rate is about 85! Lots of drafting, trying to stay honest until the packs break up. Taking the time to drink my shakes quickly while my stomach feels good, taste terrible. Drink shakes way too fast (1200 calories in about 90 minutes!). Feeling very sick to my stomach and just wanting to feel better, legs feel great, still trying to hold back on my speed, keeping it around 20mph, keep telling myself DON'T FORGET ABOUT THE MARATHON!!! making deals with myself "you can ride another 1/2 hour, then you HAVE to eat! Imagine, me not wanting to eat. This is turning out to be a very strange, wonderful and magical day. Around 3 hours, get special needs bag, only thing I want is my extra pair of socks so I don't lose them! All the food I put in there looks terrible, but I take the pretzels cause I know I need the salt. Can't eat Clif bar to save my life, 2 small snickers go down ok. MILE 80–FIRST SPIRITUAL MOMENT. Starting to feel really, really strong, like the race is just starting. Going through a wooded area, effortless, start to feel tingles and TOTALLY FEEL THE PRESENCE 0F MY DAD AND HEATHER'S GRANDMOTHER. They are so there with me, I am on the verge of crying (at mile 80 on my bike, going around 22mph). I hold back the emotion and tell them to stay with me, I will call back there presence when I need them. The feeling was so strong, I am on the verge of crying right now writing it down. I calm down and get back in the race, but periodically, I feel their spirits watching over me. 112 miles really feels easy (except for the stomach problems), I had to stop and pee so many times, I just starting peeing on the bike (glad I took those fresh socks – TMI, maybe?), My bike split is around 5:48 (probably closer to 5:43 without pee stops), much slower than I could have done, but I really want a great marathon and to finish strong.

2:30pm: Transition # 2: Much less frantic, legs are a little tight, but nowhere near as bad as I thought they would be. Take my time again, feel like I am in there for 20 minutes! Out on the run feeling great.

2:40pm: Run: Start out slow again, see Heather right at the beginning, so much love and adoration from both of us, it really gives me strength, I want to give her a great run and be strong and smiling at the finish (emotions come back again, have to hold them back), trying to get some liquid and food down, coke and water at every stop. First pee mile 1, poop at mile 4 (TMI again, took a good 3 minutes waiting for porta-potty), legs feeling great, stomach still kind of funky. Imagine if I didn't practice eating! Tough to gauge my pace, but I think I am running about 8:30's and then walking for about 1 minute in the rest stops. Feel great in the park (I love the turnaround in the park, for some reason, *I get so much strength when there is just nature and no people around)*, catch Rick at about mile 6, he is walking but looking good, he had a great bike and is doing a 5/1 run walk, I shake his hand and get great strength from seeing a friend doing well. See Kip at around mile 9, he is about 3 miles behind me (about 30min) and looking really, really strong and fast (again, very happy for him and tell him how strong he looks). Mile 10-12 stomach feeling pretty bad, one section I get real dizzy and feel like I am going to throw up, I think, this is going to be a really long, tough day if I am sick. Get some coke and pretzels at the next stop, feel much, much better–SALT IS THE KEY, NOT SUGAR AT THIS POINT!… Nothing to remember till 13.1m turnaround. I get to see Heather, and I tell her how great I am feeling, not tired yet, no real aches and pains (yet). Get special needs bag, try to eat some fig newtons, so easy to eat in training, so tough now! Get shirt cause it will be cold soon. Miles 13.1–19.1, feeling STRONGER AND STRONGER, stop to pee and put shirt on, feel like a champion and running faster and faster! Start to feel real pain around mile 15, push through it. Proceed to feel EVERY INJURY I HAVE EVER HAD! Especially "IT" band, bottom of right foot (plantar, stress fracture, etc.). It's ok, I will make it. Realize, barring any major problem, I will go under 12 hours, possibly under 11:30, beyond all my wildest expectations! Run through stop 25.1miles, start to feel emotions and allow the spirits to take me home! Want to cry when I round the corner and see the finish line (nothing like it in the world), but I stay smiling and high five the whole crowd! Run – 4:06 with a lot of stops and breaks. Hear my name and cross smiling with my hands in the air!!! Immediately look for my love and see her, within a minute, I am telling her about the presence of my dad and her grandmother and we are both totally in tears. She is so proud, I am so happy, all the training and sacrifice is worth this moment, all worth it. I love her so much and am so happy we are getting married, I wish that I could ask her again, right here and now! Life is wonderful and I am so lucky to be able to do this. I tell her, for the first time ever, instead of being sad that my dad wasn't there to see me do this, I felt like his spirit was with me the whole way and is proud (I'm crying again) of everything I have done. He is happy and at peace, (and so am I) I really feel that in my heart.

6:40pm: Finish: Basking in the moment, wait for Rick and Kip to come in, they both did great! No one is quite as emotional as I am (not surprising). TIME TO EAT AND PARTY. Try my best to make it to the midnight finish to cheer everyone in, but cold and tired, back at the hotel by 15 hours, eating Pizza, drink one beer and start shivering uncontrollably, time for bed. Can't believe I did it. Already unbelievably sore, mostly quads and calves.

WHAT AN INCREDIBLE, SPIRITUAL, PHYSICAL, MENTAL JOURNEY THIS HAS BEEN. Someday, I will do it again, but for now, I want to absorb and enjoy the moment for as long as I can!

—Rami Farouk Odeh
11/15/99
11:23:57
552nd/1500 (overall)
10th/89 ("Clydesdale" 39 and under)

Riding the mountains

When I was training for the Ironman I had some moments that I now understand as God reaching out to me in my quiet time. We did a lot of training in the North Georgia mountains, a very cool place to train. To this day my favorite climb is up the long side of Wolf Pen Gap, a climb that traverses up to about 3600 feet and took me about 20 minutes on a good day. I would love it when I would be dropped, or I would drop my training partners and just have me, the woods (this climb is surrounded by trees, no exposure) and my breathing to keep me company. I remember distinctly one climb when I was completely on my own, working hard, and a deer walked out into the road ahead of me. I kept riding (if I had gone any slower, I would have fallen over because of the steep incline) and we just stared at each other. He didn't run away—we just looked in each other's eyes and I saw God, truly. Thus began my love affair with my "deer moments"!

Deer Moments

There is something so beautiful, calm, majestic and spiritual about deer, especially seeing them in their natural habitat. They speak to my soul in a way that I can hardly articulate, maybe because they get to spend their whole lives running around the trails and woods I love so much, or maybe because they take the time to stop and check you out when you run by with those deep, dark eyes—I really don't know which. I do know that they stop me in my tracks every time I see one! Some days, when I am feeling especially good, nimble and fast on the trails, I imagine what it must feel like to be that in tune with nature—they are so, so much better than us it is not even fair!

CHAPTER 5

SOMETHING NEW

Be as healthy in body as you are strong in spirit.

3 John 1:2

I need a break

Labor Day weekend, 2007. I was finishing up another season (my 15th year) of triathlon with one of my favorite races (Callaway Gardens, GA triathlon). For a few years I had done this race as a part of a weekend away with the family, but this year it did not work out, so I just did it on my own. I remember waking up at 4:30 am that morning and for the first time *ever*, hitting the snooze before a race. Then I lay there deciding if I wanted to do this or not. Now, this might not seem strange to you, but for 15 years, for every race, to one degree or another, I had awakened excited and happy about what I was about to do. I chalked it up to a bad night's sleep and didn't think much about it, but looking back it was a definite sign. I am so glad I didn't blow off the race because it might have taken me another year to decide I needed a break from triathlons! The whole day I was just not into it. I finished and had a decent day but afterwards and on the way home I decided I needed a break and "something new"... which leads us to...

Hiking, Fall 2007

After Calloway, I took time off from swimming, biking and running for a bit. One day I headed out to a local park to go for a short hike and remembered how much I loved the trails, the woods, the quiet, nature, etc. Whenever I have had the opportunity to race on trails, it has been my favorite race that year—I love the adventure *and unexpected* nature of it, not to mention how it feels to be in the woods, not on some exposed, ugly, hot pavement! For as long as I can remember, nature has always been my place of peace and to be able to exercise at the same time seemed like a match made in heaven (of course, it is). To this day, it never ceases to amaze me how my mood and experience changes the minute I go off-road. I can be on the road, running, stressing about something, and then I turn off onto the trails and it all goes away. I am sure we all feel this to some extent or another, but the farther we get away from it the more we forget and the less likely we are to seek it out. If you are reading this right now, do me a favor and just get out in nature today and see what it does for your mood, connection, and spirit!

The first trail races, Spring 2008

After the fall and winter of 2007, realizing I could get out in nature and enjoy my wonderful trails but also get the intensity of exercise I so desperately need to clear my head, I started researching trail races—turns out there are other people who like this stuff, too! I signed up for a 10k at the Olympic Mountain biking course in Conyers to test the water and see if I liked it. It's February 2008, about 30 degrees at the start with ice and frost all over everything.

I knew this was a different world than triathlon competitions right away. The difference between road runners/triathletes and trail runners is very similar to the difference between road cyclists and mountain bikers. Road cyclists, in general, are slick and well-dressed, with their heart rate monitors, $5,000 bikes, power meters, and perfect nutrition. Mountain bikers are not so slick, with their facial hair, body piercings, and tattoos, drinking beer and sometimes smoking strange stuff after races. I knew for sure it was going to be my kind of people when a woman says at the start to her boyfriend/ husband,: "Do you think the stream crossings will be frozen over and do you think we might slip on the ice?" and he says, "Stop being such a f&%$cking girl and suck it up," and she laughs and we all take off.

I take off at a normal 10k pace and feel really good. We hit the first steep hill and everyone around me starts walking! Holy crap, I am going to win this thing—these trail runners are so out of shape they cannot run this hill. I take off and pass about 20 people, but by the time I get to the top, I am so anaerobic I really don't think I will finish the race. The 20 people I passed, plus about 100 more, pass me back in the next mile while I walk and try to recover. Lesson learned: unless you are an elite runner, if you cannot see over a hill in a trail race, especially an ultra, walk it! I actually tested this theory in a 11.5 mile race (Red Top Mountain, GA – amazing trails). One year I walked all the hills and finished in 1:44 and had a great time. The next year I ran the whole course, felt like crap, and finished 10 seconds slower than the year before, and I was in better shape the second year!

The remainder of 2008 I entered longer and longer events, building up to a trail marathon by the middle of the year. I realized early on that I got much more out of the longer distances because they really provided the quiet, alone time that I was seeking.

Confirmation, 2008

2008 was a big year for me. I got into trail running and racing and I completed my conversion to Catholicism! My wife is a "cradle Catholic" and I have always liked the Catholic religion but had never really thought about becoming one myself. I had thought that by going to an Episcopal church and taking communion there, that was "good enough" or almost the same. Boy, was I wrong.

As a couple we decided to put our kids in the local Catholic school and I started going to Mass with my wife and family just to be unified. As my son Ryan got further along in school, he started asking me specific religious questions I could not answer. I got sick of saying "ask your mother" and decided the best way to learn about the church would be to join the RCIA (Rite of Christian Initiation for Adults) program that started in the fall of 2007. Truth be told, I had never intended on going through the whole process of converting; I just figured I would take the "course" and learn all I could and then drop out before I completed it—kind of like "auditing a course" in college.

Well, about two months in, after the first initiation rite where the whole church prays for us together and after I had some of my "deal breaker" questions answered (i.e., why is it that someone who was never introduced to Christianity at all in their lives can go to Hell) in a way that made me understand, I fell in love with the church. I enjoyed the whole experience. Heather and I actually got "re-married" by our priest on June, 14, 2008 (now I have two anniversaries to remember, whew!) and on Easter Sunday, 2008, I was welcomed fully into the Catholic Church!

CHAPTER 6

THE TRAIL LESS TRAVELED

For the Lord your God is going with you! He will fight for you against your enemies, and he will give you victory!

Deuteronomy 20:4

Daddy time

In October of 2009, I spent four days with my daughter Hana while my wife and son were at a wedding in California. We went to the park, and the movies, and she came with me to work. On Saturday, I brought Hana to a gymnastics birthday party. Hana was going through a phase where she wanted to avoid "new people," so she didn't want to go. This had nothing to do with her ability, since she was probably one of the most able four-year-olds at almost all sports (she just learned to ride her bike with no training wheels in about 30 minutes)! When we walk into the party she starts crying and says, "I don't want to do this." Well, the easy road (the one most traveled) would have been to give in and go home. With some advice from mom via text messages, I stayed with her and slowly got her to engage and she did great. The message: The more difficult trail is the one God wants us to follow and always, always the right one.

Fast forward, I am dropping Hana off that night at her friend's house to sleep over so I can run a trail marathon in the morning. We have dinner and she is doing great with her best 10-year-old buddy, Julianna "T". I ask her if it is OK for Daddy to leave and she says "sure!" Now, this is the easy road as it is much easier to sleep in my own bed, make breakfast, shower, etc. in my own, empty house at 5 am for a race. The more difficult trail would have been to stay over and make sure she was OK (would have been the right thing to do).

Anyway, I assume the family will put her to bed around 10 pm and if she is having trouble, I will drive back over. No call so I head off to sleep at 10:30 pm, looking at 6.5 hours sleep before running the toughest trail marathon in my life. Phone, of course, rings at 11:30 pm, and she is crying and "wants Daddy". Easy road: go get her, change my plans, sleep in and do my run another day. Tough trail (with help from mom on the phone): leave her there and hope for the best. Get a text at 2:30 am that she is asleep and OK. I get about 4 hours sleep. Shut off my alarm, run late for the race—the whole way there and the whole run I am worrying about her. Never would have happened if I just stayed there (tougher trail).

Race Day

The race that I was signed up for was the "Mystery Mountain Marathon", I had done the 12 mile option year before and had sworn I would never do the marathon, because the shorter 12 mile was the toughest "short" trail race I had ever done—12 miles took me 2hours, 15minutes! I decided to do this marathon as a brutal training day for my 40 mile race. It was so difficult that I never even felt like I was running—I was either climbing a 25% (or more) grade or sliding down a terrible, rocky, rooted logging trail. There were so many times I wanted to quit but I continued and finished with a 5:42 time—slower than my first trail marathon by almost an hour.

I really cannot put into words how hard this course was. Two days after the race, if anyone so much as touched my quads, I would punch him! There were some beautiful scenes early in the race (and many more later in the race) but there was no way I could appreciate them. I had to call on God, Dad, etc. very early (three hours in) to get me through. I got to a rest stop at 2hours, 45minutes and we were only at 12.6 miles, *omg*!!!

Lesson: Choose the tougher trail, it is *always* God's plan and is the right thing to do.

PART TWO

It's not that I have already reached this goal or have already become perfect. But I keep pursuing it, hoping somehow to embrace it just as I have been embraced by the Messiah Jesus.

Philippians 3;12

CHAPTER 7

FIRST ULTRA, MOUNTAIN MIST 2009

Yet those who wait for the LORD will gain new strength; they will mount up with wings like eagles, they will run and not get tired, they will walk and not become weary.

Isaiah 40:31

Training

I started trail running in October of 2007 because I was burnt out on triathlon. Trail running brought me back to my motocross roots and had a very strong spiritual and peaceful bent to it that I really needed in my life then. I started in February of '08 with an off-road 10k and I was hooked! In my typical Type A fashion, by May of '08, I had run my first off- road marathon. To give you an idea of how much harder off-road running courses are than road running, my last road marathon time was 3:36 against 12,000 runners. In my first off-road, I ran 4:55 (second in my age group) against 150 runners – quite a change!

Then I decided to do an Ultra! An ultra marathon is anything longer than 26.2 miles. I tried to run one step longer than the finish line at the off-road marathon but I was informed this did not count! I decided to do the Mountain Mist 50k in Huntsville, Alabama, mostly because of the description: "The toughest 50k in the South." They did not lie! See the email from the race director three days before the race:

> "Mountain Mist is trail running in its finest form. No one is ever let down—just shut down, beaten up, broken and left bleeding. You first timers beware, this course may cause you bodily harm. Even though you have entered the race and paid the fee...YOU CAN STILL BACK OUT! No one will laugh at you, just tell them your family still needs you and you want to continue running in the future, they'll understand! Otherwise, 'know your limits and then completely ignore them.'"

The training was not easy: I slowly worked up to a 4.5 hour off-road run, walk, and shuffle and figured I was ready. I definitely learned that I do not run anywhere near the distances these people do (I was doing about 30-40 miles total a week, while they run that in most weekends and up to 150 miles a week). They consider a 50k a "short race" and use it for training for their 50 mile, 100k or 100 mile runs! Intriguing to say the least, but I am not quite there…yet!

Race Day

I drove to Alabama Friday afternoon, checked into the hotel and went to check into the race. You have to check in the night before, the morning of, and when you get to and when you leave all the rest stops. I suppose they don't want to lose anyone 15 miles from nowhere! Then off to listen to a motivational speaker brought in for the race, David Horton, famous in the Ultra Running community. He has held the record for running the Application Trail, the Pacific Coast Trail and…. racing across America (think Forrest Gump). Great quote to remember: "Suffering ceases to be suffering when it finds meaning." Had a good dinner and got to bed early.

Woke up at 5:45 am. It's rainy and 38 degrees, perfect! Spent the morning eating, stretching, pooping (fellow racers understand this all too well), and smiling—feeling truly blessed to be able to even attempt this! I waited in the lodge with the other 339 nuts until two minutes before the start, lined up and took off, very, very slowly!

Unless you get out front right away, this kind of race is very frustrating because you follow single file, at someone else's pace, for up to 60 minutes before the pack breaks up. I figured with 31 miles ahead of me, no worries about starting slow. The first 10k was pretty uneventful (except for sliding down a frozen stream at mile 2); my body felt amazing (keep in mind I outweigh 99% of the other racers by about 30-50lbs). In fact the first three hours, up to mile 17 were actually easy!

At one point I thought to myself, "this is kind of a disappointment, nowhere near as hard as advertised." Bad thought…bad, bad thought. I kept thinking of how weird it is at the beginning of a trail race to be surrounded by nature at its best, feeling wonderful, but all you can do is look down at the ground two feet in front of you to make sure you don't trip and so you end up staring at the shoes of the guy running ahead of you. For the first three hours, I was singing songs in my head – mostly the last song I heard, over and over, but then my mind went completely quiet and I was totally in the moment for the rest of the race. My efforts at practicing how to find the feeling of being close to God and holding on to that feeling were having a positive effect. I was also practicing staying in a place of optimism and a feeling of being truly blessed, even when I had down moments, which I knew would be coming…

The going gets tough

OK, now the race really begins. At hours 3-4 (mile 16-21), things started to get tougher. I realized that we were going up and down a lot more because the temperature kept changing. We ran through every eco-system you could imagine: green forests, barren power line-laced fields, and an actual cave where it was pitch black. By the way, the rest stops at these races are *amazing*! The volunteers rock, the food is great, and since I am not really "racing", I can hang around for a couple of minutes and take a break, kind of like the rest stops in an organized bike ride. This was also the best organized trail race I have ever done—hats off to the race director!

After hour 4, things started to get really interesting. First of all, I became totally uninterested in food and drink. Up to this point I had been fueling very well, taking 1 gel and an Accelerade every 30 minutes and as much as I could stomach at the rest stops. Now my body just said it was done, so I went with it. I decided to just drink as much as I could and take in Coke at the rest stops. If my body was saying "no," I would listen, figuring if I could keep my heart rate down, I would use body fat for fuel anyway.

I started looking forward to the steep uphills! The downhills were so rocky and dangerous you couldn't really run and the flats kicked my ass because my legs were getting so tired. At this point I tried something new and took an Aleve (I know, nothing new on race day, but I figured, nothing risked, nothing gained) and it really felt good after hour 5 when it kicked in. I had also taken an Imodium in the morning, following advice from other ultras with digestive issues like me—great move!

Throughout the race I had kept hearing about the "waterline trail" and the "waterfall climb;" now we turned a corner after a very easy section and there it was: a trail straight up a mountain, probably 15% grade or steeper, for at least 15-20 minutes—I loved it! Then we turned again and in front of me was a frozen waterfall that we had to climb! Remember, this is about 5 hours into the race after 24 miles of running, *and* after the steepest hill of the race. This section made me think, if I could drop about 30 lbs., I would really love climbing mountains! It was so tough and even scary, actually climbing (with all four limbs) up a muddy, frozen waterfall. I had to stop, which I never do, halfway up to take a break. I can't describe how great it felt to get to the top, but running again after that really, really sucked!

At the next rest stop, at mile 25, I thought, jokingly, of course, if I can run a 44 minute 10k now, I will break 6 hours (it ended up taking me 84 minutes!). The next four miles were absolute hell. The downhills were so steep and covered with rocks, the flats were jagged big rocks, there were no uphills for a break, and my legs were completely dead. My body wanted nothing to do with any gel, jelly bean, or sugary substance whatsoever, even though that's exactly what it needed.

AKA: Goat Boy

Then, at mile 27, I turned my ankle so badly I saw stars and I thought, "Oh well, if my race is over, at least I ran longer than a marathon." I surprised myself by recovering within two minutes. All that training really paid off (endorphins and Aleve didn't hurt.). Finally, we got to the last uphill, very tough but a welcome change from the rocky downhills. From there it was about a mile up to the last rest stop at 29.2 miles, and then only 1.8 miles of flat, easy trails to the finish!

OK, here is where it gets *really* weird: I look up ahead and see a large black and white animal cross the trail. I get closer and it is lying down in the grass, a huge-ass *wild goat*! It looked at me, I looked at it, and we both tried to decide if I was hallucinating! Still waiting on confirmation from the race director that there are mountain goats up there. If not, I'll blame it on severe glycogen depletion. Then, at mile 30 or so, I look down and the pack I was carrying with my car key in it was open, who knows for how long. I was so freaked out, thinking what a bummer it would be if I had to break my car window to get to my warm dry clothes. God was with me again and the key was still there, thank the Lord!

Believe it or not, 1.8 miles is a long way after 29.2. I had to walk a lot, but was actually able to sprint the finish! My time was 6:39, 148th overall out of 340 and 44th in my age group. The only mistake I made the whole weekend was not getting the hotel for another night and having to drive home for 4 hours to get home. But, on the upside, it was great to get home to my family and a big meal and homemade brownies!

Postscript: the goat was confirmed to be real by race director and many other racers!

CHAPTER 8

THANKFULNESS

But one thing I do: Forgetting what is behind and straining toward what is ahead, I press on toward the goal to win the prize for which God has called me heavenward in Christ Jesus.

Philippians 3:13-14

Planning Ultra 2

The decision to do my next Ultra, the Pine Mountain 40 miler, goes way back to about when the soreness left my legs from the Mountain Mist 50k in 2009. I wanted to do another ultra, and actually signed up for two more 50k races in the spring, but the training was not there and the logistics and finances were too tough with the current economic situation. So I decided to sign up for this race to end the year on a good note with another ultra and to learn something new about myself and my relationship with the Lord. My training was good: it was not as consistent as for Mountain Mist, but I was able to do more long runs and more back-to-back long runs. I also ran the toughest off-road marathon I have ever done (in terms of terrain and elevation change) in October, so I felt I was fairly ready, as ready as you can ever be for a distance you have never attempted. Some of you might be thinking, "it is only 9 miles longer than the race he did in January," but considering I probably couldn't have run another step after that race, 9 miles is an eternity (actually, 2 hours and 16 minutes more, to be exact).

I had made a decision not to taper as much as in the past, just because I was recovering well and it really doesn't seem like the trails need as much recovery as the road. Plus this training is obviously therapy for me and I wanted to keep up the intensity level of my training runs so I wouldn't get antsy (or drive my family crazy) as a result of cutting back on training for a month before this race. But then, a week before the race, I got a terrible cold. Normally, I shake a cold in 2-3 days so I was not worried, but this was a different animal altogether.

The cold forced me to taper back on training runs, so I figured it was God's way of slowing me down. I did very little the week before except walk and run about 30 minutes a day and try to sleep as much as possible. The Friday before the race I still had a bad cold and no voice—what a way to head into a 40 mile running race! We spent the weekend down at the race site, in a little cabin with friends. Focusing on getting better took my mind off the race almost entirely, so I wasn't nervous or anxious at all. Silver lining to everything, I suppose. We had a great time chilling with the family, fishing with the kids, and enjoying nice dinners with new friends, something we don't do as much anymore, so it was a blessing. My friend's son and I were both celebrating birthdays: he was turning 7, and I was turning 47. Humbling. Also, the guy we were staying with is one of the best trail runners in the Southeast and would probably win. That was more humble pie, really in line with the theme of the weekend!

Race day

Went to bed around 9 and got up at 4:30 am. At the race site it was 28 degrees but not much wind and no rain or snow. I was completely calm and in the moment, ready to start the race as soon as I could find my friend and coach, Matt "R". Matt, a very accomplished triathlete and endurance sport coach, had decided to run this race "to see what his clients are going through." This was his first trail race and he didn't train much for it, but keep in mind, Matt had the ability to probably be in the top 5 in this thing if he wanted.

Originally, we had planned to run the first 30 miles together and then whoever was feeling better (that would certainly be him) would take off, but he decided after 10 miles he was having so much fun (and I was such a great conversationalist!) he would stay with me. Actually, I think he was worried I wouldn't make it and he didn't want that on his "client resume." Now, this was completely a new experience in trail running for me. All of my races had been done solo, 99 percent with an ipod on, in my own head, talking to no one. I wasn't sure how it was going to go, but I decided to go with it and really didn't give it much thought to how different it would be.

There are only about 120 people in this race, so it thinned out very quickly and it was just me and Matt. I was excited and very happy because my family was planning to meet me at the first or second aid station (about every 3-5 miles). What a spiritual lift it is to see the smiling faces of your family every hour or so! The first four hours of the race were actually very easy, joking and laughing with Matt. We laughed that we used to do "boys' nights" and "boys' trips," but now we need to run 40 miles to have some "guy time."

There was a moment before mile 20 where I started to see "water" around the corners of my eyes and wondered if I was going blind like I did as a kid due to heat stroke (long story for another book), even though it was about 40 degrees. Matt had noticed that every time the sun came out, I stopped talking and had a really bad patch. At the next aid station another runner heard me say to Heather, "I may be going blind" and told me that same thing happened to him and his doc had advised him "to stop doing ultra marathons." Like that would ever happen! But I did start to put together some pieces: heat stroke as a kid, soaking in ice water between motocross races, having to dress warmer in winter races and then taking clothes off, heat rash on my face after every long training session. I realized I had a serious thermo-regulatory issue, something I would really need to work on if I wanted to go longer in this sport.

Trouble

After five hours, the race really started to get difficult for me. Matt was a great coach and very supportive but I was experiencing many more lows than highs. I was having trouble with any type of food and not joking at aid stations like I normally do. My legs felt great, but I felt an overwhelming sense of exhaustion all over my body and, especially, in my mind and spirit. It was weird to be able to talk to someone about this, as I normally just process this all in my head since I usually run solo. Another thing about having a "pacer" which is really what Matt was doing for me (I am not even sure if he got his heart rate over 100 the whole race) is that he kept track of the time for me.

The race now became a real struggle (with some short, good running patches on the downhills) from aid station to aid station. At points I am walking about a 60 minute mile and thinking, "I cannot finish" and then I am running all out (on autopilot, not sure where I am or where my feet are landing) and it is probably a 12 minute mile! Anyone who has run one of these will understand that you have such incredible highs and lows. After a bit Matt starts calculating what pace we will have to keep to finish in under 9 hours, but at this point I am just happy to make the 10.5 hour cutoff!

What a learning experience for me to be in the position of "client" as he is pushing me, motivating me, trying to get more out of me For so many years I have been on the other side as a personal trainer, running races with so many people who were not as fit as me! Humbling and wonderful at the same time to be able to let go. I make the mistake of looking at my watch with about a mile to go and it says 4:02 pm (yes, we have been "running" since 7 am) so I say, it's over, let's just cruise in. He keeps pushing me, though, even harder, and I have no idea why but I am delirious at this point and just want to finish. Turns out my watch is wrong—the finishing clock says 8:55.

I run in with my family—what an amazing feeling! I really have never been so incredibly tired in any race; Ironman was not even close (of course, I was in much better shape then).

My connection with God was this: Thankfulness. I was so thankful for my life and for my blessings, and so happy that my family was together and healthy and happy. So thankful to have a good friend like Matt willing to sacrifice his potential race finish to spend a day of "boy time" and fellowship with me and to motivate me to finish something so hard. Thankful for the blissful and peaceful feeling I had all that night and the next day. Thankful that there were others that wanted to promote and participate in this new sport I have found. Thankful that I could still afford to do this, that our business was still running well enough to allow me to have a weekend off. Thankful that my body could do this type of thing, and my mind could push me through. Thankful for the tough times during the race (and life) that teach us so much about ourselves. Thankful for God's nature that was such an inspiration during the race.

I have a truly blessed life and this race really clarified that fact. My pledge today is to stay as much in this space of thankfulness as I can and use this memory to bring me back when life and circumstances try to pull me out of it.

CHAPTER 9

AN UNPLANNED DAY "OFF"

My flesh and my heart may fail, but God is the strength of my heart and my portion forever.

Psalm 73:26

That sinking feeling

Long distance running has its ups and downs and so does real life. 2008 began a down period for me. From 2008-2010, in spite of doing all our efforts at couples counseling, I felt like our marriage was not working well. At the same time, we were trying to deal with the biggest financial challenges in our business in our 11 year history, by far. Our yearly revenue was down 50%, *and* our operating costs had doubled, due to a recent expansion.

I was really struggling to improve our marriage. I felt like I had tried my best over the past two years, doing many things that did not feel natural to me, but I did them because they were suggested by a book or a therapist. Even so, things had not gotten any better.

Keep in mind, my vision for our marriage (and my career) was pretty mainstream and, until 2008, I felt like we were doing great. Our business had been growing at a pace of 30% per year from 1999–2008. That was also the year I converted to Catholicism. Since 2008 had been such an up, I wasn't ready for the down that came next. I suppose, after all those years of distance running, having experienced that up, down, up, down pattern over and over again, I should have been ready, but some lessons just have to be learned over and over again.

So, for the next two years I struggled, praying every day the same simple prayers:

- Thank you, Lord, for all my blessings.
- Please allow me to follow your path every day and be the best version of myself I can be.
- Please give me the strength to keep perspective every day as I know there are so many people who have it so much worse than I do and I should not complain about what is going on in my life right now.

On one particular Tuesday, I left our therapy appointment completely exhausted emotionally and physically. I had no motivation to go into work and do accounting and book work (a big part of my Tuesday routine) and face the red ink. On the way back, I decided to go for a run to clear my head. I went to a local trail and planned on doing one hour. 100 feet into the run I was not motivated to do that either (very, very rare). I turned around to go back to my car, not sure what I was going to do next (strange behavior since I almost always have a plan).

I changed my mind, deciding that maybe a two hour run would do me better. Then, I realized that this lack of decision was part of my problem. I checked my day planner to confirm that I had no appointments for the rest of the day (lots work to do, but no appointments I would have to cancel), so I decided, really decided, to take the day off from work and go for a long run and see where that put me. I instantly felt better, not back to normal, but already on the right path.

Give it my best

Driving to Kennesaw Mountain, one of my favorite places to do long trail runs (there is a 16-17 mile loop that is fairly easy and I almost always see deer there), I thanked the Lord for the blessing of having the choice to do what I was doing that day. Imagine me calling my boss at a large company and saying, "I am taking day off to go trail running"!

I got to the mountain parking lot at noon; it was already about 90 degrees but I really wasn't planning on this so I didn't think about it at the time. I ran and processed, ran and processed, ran and prayed. Ninety minutes in I was feeling awesome, a bit hot but no problems (it was probably 95 by then but the humidity was so low I didn't feel bad at all). At two hours exhaustion and heat hit me. It was time to suffer. This is *exactly* what I wanted and needed.

I stopped processing, stopped worrying, and stopped "looping"–what I call the OCD method of repeating your issue in your head over and over without coming to any type of conclusion or solution. I was starting to become "raw". I needed this so badly. My mind cleared and all I thought about was one step in front of the other, getting back to the car, cold water, cold shower, ice bath. My "reptile brain" had taken over, just like I needed it to.

I finished the run completely spent. Three hours (17 miles) of trail running in 90 plus degree heat left me with barely enough energy to change and drive home. After cold drinks, food, and an ice bath, however, my mind was clear and I realized what I needed to do (at least for now) with my marriage and my business. I learned my lesson yet again: God is with us and speaking to us all the time, but we need to clear our heads to hear him. Some of us do this with meditation, some do it with reading or music, and others (especially anxiety ridden, type-A, slightly OCD people like myself) do it with intense, outdoor exercise!

I decided to give my marriage and my business my best possible effort for as long as I could to see if I can follow God's plan. I coach people all the time with their exercise and weight loss goals and I tell them that most people "quit the race" (whatever that race may be) 100 yards from the finish line, especially if they cannot see the finish line! I do not want to give up without knowing that I have given it my very best effort!

Whew.

CHAPTER 10

SILENCE, SOLITUDE AND SUFFERING

Therefore, since we are surrounded by such a great cloud of witnesses, let us throw off everything that hinders and the sin that so easily entangles. And let us run with perseverance the race marked out for us, fixing our eyes on Jesus, the pioneer and perfecter of faith. For the joy set before him he endured the cross, scorning its shame, and sat down at the right hand of the throne of God. Consider him who endured such opposition from sinners, so that you will not grow weary and lose heart.

Hebrews 12:1-3

Broken promise

I awoke at 4:30 am on Sunday, 10/10/10 with some trepidation and nervousness, something I had not experienced in a while. Due to the economy and the fact that I do not enjoy competing in the summer, I had not "raced" since February and this trail marathon would be only my second race of the year: it had been twenty years since I had done only two races in a year.

In 2008 I had run the 12 mile option of the Mystery Mountain Marathon ("MMM") and had sworn I would *never, ever* do the marathon option. It is a brutal course, mostly up and down (one GPS measurement has it at *15,000* ft. of elevation change in 26.2 miles – ouch!) and along the side of a mountain near the Tennessee border in Georgia. I was sore for a week after the 12 mile option! Naturally, even after swearing I would never run the marathon option, I had gone ahead and signed up to run it in 2009, mostly because I was training for my first 40 mile race and this course looked like strong training opportunity. I finished the marathon in 5 hours and 42 minutes and swore I would *never, ever* do it again.

So, of course, I signed up for the 2010 marathon! Somehow, I must have forgotten about the 15,000 foot elevation change, a large amount of which occurs between miles 18 and 22. There are also sections of the run that are very, very rocky with some of the steepest downhill terrain I have ever run: my quads were so sore I had to walk down stairs sideways for a week. Yet, here I am getting ready to run it again. My reason for changing my mind again?

It would be a great time of year—think fall color—to race, but I forgot I would have to train for 12 weeks in the summer *before* the race. It would be good training to finish the year and kick off my training for my first 50 miler in March of 2011. In spite of 8 years of college (4 years in Grad School), I am really not very smart. But I did get something out of the whole experience, in spite of breaking that promise to never, ever, run "MMM" again. I learned the lessons of Silence, Suffering and Solitude.

Silence

I ran the first 11 miles with a good friend. It was his first trail race, so I was able to keep him company at the beginning but then he needed to keep a slow pace and I had to pick up my pace in order to finish before the real heat set in. After I left him, I put on my Ipod to enjoy four more hours of music and trails, and, it *died*! Now, this might not seem like a big deal, but I do almost all my running with music and there were not many people to talk to during this race, so this kind of freaked me out! I tried everything to fix it, but it just was not in God's plan for me to listen to music on this day. Actually, the silence and the sounds of nature were very nice, changing the experience for me. Not that silence is better than music— it's just different.

Suffering

It was hot, really hot. Last year it was freezing and the race was still, by far, the hardest trail I had ever run. This year I was in shorts and a short-sleeved shirt, and I was sweating after just a half mile! It actually warmed up to over 85 degrees, not good running weather for me. I get overheated very easily. Although I was in fantastic aerobic shape, having done plenty of long runs, I was *not* in good shape for those hills. Nothing can prepare you for this course unless you go up and train on it! I felt completely fine until mile 18.5, but those last 7.5 miles took me almost two hours to complete!

I couldn't enjoy a bit of the beautiful scenery since my body was just suffering, suffering, suffering, and begging for the day to be over. I came as close as I ever have to dropping out of a race at mile 22. At that point I just calculated that if I walked the whole rest of the way I could still finish in under the eight hour cut-off. I used this time to try to connect to the Lord, struggling to focus on the blessing that I am able to do this. I was wearing a bracelet to remind me of a 13-year-old in our school who has brain cancer, so I could look at that and focus attention on him. God stayed with me, but it was very, very hard, especially as I fought through heat exhaustion.

Solitude

Because of the extreme nature of this race, there were only about 80 people in the marathon so there were many, many times when I ran long stretches alone. I discovered that I really enjoy solitude when I am training and feeling good, but when I feel like crap, it really helps to have someone to talk to, to suffer with, and even just to walk with. I realized at one point that outside of running in this race, I probably had nothing else in common with the guy I was walking along with, but it just felt so good to have another human being there with me!

Although—at one point when I was very, very low and I could tell he was feeling good, I was about ready to push him off the side of the mountain. Luckily that feeling passed!

I finished the race, with a time of 6 hours and 4 minutes, 22 minutes slower than last year, but still 28th overall. Felt absolutely exhausted, burnt out, miserable. Had a cold Coke, jumped into a freezing lake, and felt wonderful within 5 minutes. It's amazing how your mood can change instantly when one of these things are over.

Note to self: Don't you dare sign up for this race again. Unless you...

- lose 20 lbs.
- do some serious hill training beforehand
- forget about how hard the 4 mile uphill section is

10 years old on my first minibike. I am sure I
crashed right after this impressive wheelie

Me and John "D" showing off my first motocross bike and
the impressive Toyota Corolla and trailer. We would get
3 bikes on that thing and then fit 3 riders, 2 parents and
all of our stuff in the trunk. No idea how we did it.

In the corral waiting for practice (I am number "27m") – never before
and never after as out of my head nervous as I was at that moment

My first and only (amateur) supercross race. Looks impressive
cause all the spectators were in front of this jump!

Race stub from my first ever 10k race (18 years old). Speed
(and handwriting) has not changed much in 32+ years!

What I had to show after my 14 year motocross "career"

WALT DISNEY WORLD MARATHON
January 16, 1994
Marathon Foto

Disney marathon 1994: gotta love the short shorts and 'stach!

ST. ANTHONY'S TAMPA BAY
TRIATHLON-APRIL 25, 1993
Action Sports of America

Triathlon in 1993. Seriously, everyone dressed like this at triathlons in the 80's and 90's. I swear! Yes, that is a colored-flower speedo – ouch.

Finishing my one and only Ironman. I am looking
up and smiling about 2 seconds after this.

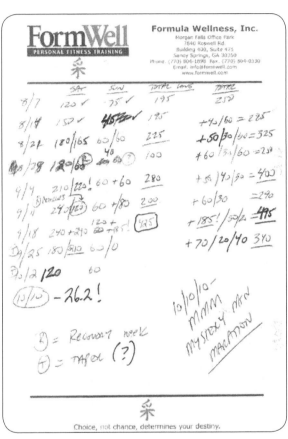

Training log for first trail marathon

Training log for first 40 miler

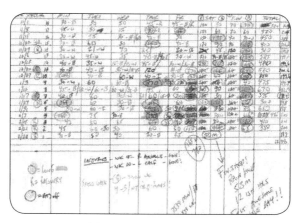

Training log for 53 miler

Happy running at Red Top Mountain

Happy finish in front of waterfall

Happy with Kids on top of Kennesaw Mountain

Double Rainbow on the way to a mountain run:
can you say good message from God?

One of my favorite moments, the sunrise through the clouds and trees!

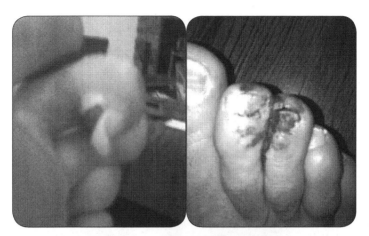

The wonderful benefits of trail running

What an Iroman Swim looks like. 1800 people spread out over 2.4 miles of the Gulf of Mexico. Not much "noise" in my head at this moment!

This is how much a 200 lb trail runner eats in 53 miles of running!

Happy to get first Red Bull and M&M's at
mile 20 of 53. Breakfast of champions!

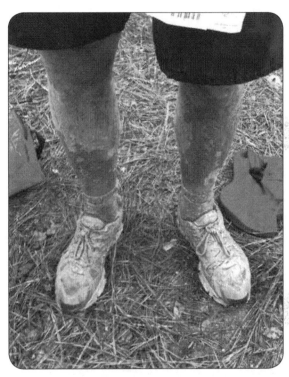

What your feet look like after running in rain
and mud for 12 hours!

What your clothes look like after same!

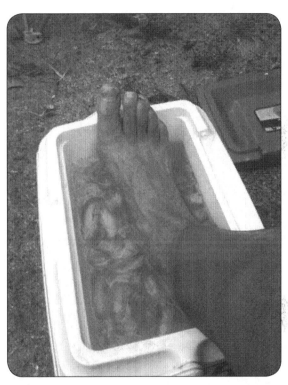

Treating my 15 year long Achilles injury. Pain is just an emotional response to a real or perceived trauma!

Ryan's first race – we are BOTH nervous!

The approach trail to Springer Mountain (the terminus of the AT) – one of my favorite runs, this is right after a huge fire that only burned one side of the trail

A very happy family down at the beach!

Our fitness club in full swing!

Perhaps a reason I have a tough time staying under 200lbs???

CHAPTER 11

THE 50 MILE DECISION

The LORD God is my strength, and he will make my
feet like hinds' feet, and he will make me to walk upon
mine high places.

Habakkuk 3:19

100,000 steps

If the journey of a 1000 steps (or in this case 100,000) begins
with a single step, then my decision to attempt a 50 mile
trail run is that first step. In November of 2010 I began to
seriously train for my first 50 mile trail run, scheduled for
3/5/2011. When I ran my first trail marathon (the one I
promised myself never to run again) and I realized that the
traditional 26.2 mile was not the only possibility—there were
opportunities for even greater suffering just waiting for me!—
then, of course, I was hooked! I had slowly worked my way up
to running a 40 mile race (not really sure if you could call it

"running") and now I decided I wanted to complete a 50 mile race before I turned 50 (which was still two years away but better safe than sorry). A further inducement—the unwritten agreement in the Ultra-running community that the "real" ultra-marathons begin at 50 miles, since that's about when you begin to hallucinate!

This may not seem like much of a stretch after completing 40 miles, but, trust me, every mile after 26.2 gets longer and longer and tougher and tougher. For example, although I ran my first trail marathon in 4:50, I ran my first 50k in 6:39 (almost 2 hours more to run 6 miles farther) and I ran the 40 mile race in 8:55 (another 2.5 hours to run 9 miles)! At this pacing, I would be very happy to finish 50 miles in under 12 hours. That's right, this newest goal will have me running dirt trails in North Georgia from 6 am till after 6pm!

After my trail marathon on 10/10/10 I had decided, or more accurately, my body had decided for me, that I needed some time off before I began my next training cycle. At the time, I figured a week would do it but somehow, that one week stretched to three weeks of no running, minimal training, eating whatever I wanted, and drinking...well, whatever I wanted...fun for a bit, but getting pretty old by Halloween. I have to remember to be very careful taking time off after a brutal event—it is not easy to get back into the habit of running daily! Anyway, I put together an 18 week training program that progressively adds miles during the week and slowly increases the back-to-back long weekend runs. It's three weeks of tough training, a week of recovery, then the same again for four cycles, and then it's race time!

My goal was to drop about 10 pounds; more would have been better but I wasn't sure how my body would react to the increase in training. I'd end up running six days per week and then 5-6 hours on Saturday and another 2-3 hours on Sunday, so I was not too concerned about cutting calories to achieve the weight loss.

As always, my first and most important goal was to obtain personal and spiritual lessons from the journey toward my goal, counting my blessings daily that I had the ability, time and desire to complete such a goal. The next goal was to finish, just that. And then, if I were blessed to finish, I wanted to finish feeling strong (or as strong as you can feel after 50 miles). And, if I were blessed to finish strong, I would want to finish in under 12 hours.

Time for "real" training

For the first week of training, I did some cardio each day. Monday I biked 30 minutes, Tuesday I walked on treadmill 40 minutes, Wednesday I went for a short run, and so on. I ended up with 320 minutes of very, very easy cardio and two weight workouts. My "long" run for the week was 70 minutes of easy trails. I also did some road running, which reminded me how my body does not like road running, but it is easier to do a quick road run than it is to do a trail run when you don't have a lot of time. One morning I did a coffee run: 45 minutes to a meeting at a coffee shop (included coffee and a whole grain bagel), then another 45 minutes home!

I was 204 lbs. and 15% body fat, working toward my goal to drop about 1 lb. per week of mostly body fat, keeping as much muscle tissue as I can along the way. Unfortunately, I know enough about human physiology (just enough to be dangerous as they say) to understand that when I begin to run more than 500 minutes per week, keeping all my muscle will be impossible

I Went "cold turkey" on simple sugar products, starting the day after Halloween (after eating about 400 of my kids' candies so this was not an easy detox). I was eating Chia seeds every morning with a protein smoothie. I began to cut my calories a bit when I started teaching our companies' weight loss program, so I could experience the program along with the participants!

Easy, outdoor exercise

One weekend in fall 2011 I traveled to NY with my son, Ryan (9 years old at the time). I can really get to know the children a lot better when it's one on one! Ryan and I got up Saturday and decided to walk to town for breakfast. What I noticed on this short walk is that every time Ryan and I walk somewhere, even if it is only for 20-30 minutes, we interact better, are in the moment more, are more relaxed and see "God's Nature," as my son so eloquently puts it, everywhere we look. When we drive somewhere or spend time indoors, we have fun, but we are more stressed and not in the moment—typical dudes.

The next weekend I had the day alone with my daughter, Hana. Now, Hana is much more like me: constantly moving, addicted to sugar, and anxious when trying anything she is not comfortable with. She is also a sweetheart and absolutely gorgeous, just like her dad (oops, the humility lessons I learned running the Pine Mountain 40miler must have just worn off)! We decided to go to the park and hang out as we had a free day together. Now, on the way to the park I was a bit anxious because I had not run or worked out that day and thus was not really in the moment. Once we got there, she played for a bit while I read a book. Then she decided to "run the trails" with Dad! There is a very nice, one mile trail at this park that I walk and run with the kids and the dog sometimes. I really thought we would walk most of it but she ran, and ran fast for almost the whole mile (in her Ruby Red slippers). Once we were done, we both lay down on the grass and looked up at the sky, totally content and in the moment. Looking at clouds, appreciating the beautiful weather and our time together.

I found out it doesn't need to be an intense workout, or a 30 mile run, to help me quiet my mind and be in the moment with God. Anything that breaks me out of the daily "grind," stops me from being distracted, and lets me appreciate the moment can help! A 30 minute walk with my son. A one mile trail run with my daughter. Amazing how little we need sometimes to relax and get focused on what is really important!

CHAPTER 12

CHANGES

Physical training is good, but training for godliness is much better, promising benefits in this life and in the life to come.

1 Timothy

The Stranger

Well, we all have a face, that we hide away forever, and we take them to show ourselves when everyone is gone. Some are satin, some are steel, some are silk and some are leather.... they're the faces of the Stranger but we love to try them on.

I had been singing that song for a week (not sure I've got the lyrics right—forgive me, Billy Joel!) and I could not figure out why I kept singing it. Finally, during a 20 mile run in the cold and snow, it all became clear. When I started at 8 am at Kennesaw Mountain, it was warm and rainy. I had taken some extra clothes that I really didn't need because I had heard the temperature might drop, thank *God*! The first 90 minutes of the 17 mile loop were actually warm but, as the morning progressed, it dropped about 20 degrees and the wind picked up, so, by the time I crested Kennesaw Mountain at about three hours into the run, it was snowing. I couldn't feel my hands or legs (I was in shorts), but I was as happy as I have been in ages!

What does this all have to do with "The Stranger," you ask? Well, I think I realized my "stranger" is *a pure runner*. I have been running on and off, mostly on, for 35+ years. When I started running as a teen, it was to get in shape for motocross.

When I got to college, I continued running a bit but then I got into weight lifting and completely changed my body. Since starting to compete in triathlons in 1992, I had tried to keep a balance between skinny triathlete/runner and buff bodybuilder, but it wasn't really working.

Even though off-road ultra-running had re-sparked my love of training, I kept on trying to lift heavy weights and maintain all of my muscle mass. All the suffering I had endured running my last ultra finally made me realize that I couldn't keep carrying the bodybuilder's extra weight if I really wanted to compete in my new sport. It was time to let go of the bodybuilder and embrace "The Stranger."

I decided to allow my body to "morph" into a pure runner for the upcoming 50 mile race and see how I did both psychologically and physically. You see, I really enjoyed having some muscle on my body when I would go to the beach but what I *really* enjoyed was the feeling of running long distances in nature without pain or struggling due to excess body weight. So, I guess what you could say is my public persona was a weight lifter who tried to run long distances but my "stranger face" that I really wanted to try on was a Pure Runner.

I was able to drop about 11 lbs. (broke 200 lbs. for the first time since 1999) and was consistently running/cross training 400+ minutes per week. I had to keep doing weight training 2x per week to maintain my core strength, prevent injuries, and try to lose body fat while maintaining lean mass. This program was designed specifically for running performance, not for aesthetic body shaping.

With my 50 mile run about 14 weeks away, I was feeling so fine that I started surfing the really "dark side" of Ultra Running, 100 mile races. More on this later...

Silver lining

God had plans and I had plans and they were sometimes close, but mostly far apart. However, the more I listen to him and "let go" and accept his will (Thy Will Be Done), the more I come to understand and appreciate his infinite wisdom and love. On this particular day, I had planned to sleep in and run whenever I got up, even though the message from the Lord had been for a while to get up early every day and run before starting anything else. Every time I did that, I had a great day and was able to hear him and follow his path. Almost every time I didn't do that, it felt good (temporary pleasure, i.e.,

Satan) for a bit and then my anxiety was high and my day was very far off my spiritual road!

Anyway, on Saturday afternoon it came to my attention that my wife had a brunch to go to on Sunday morning and I would have to take Ryan to his school function, so I needed to be done with my Sunday run by noon (instead of sleeping in). Now, for a normal human being, sleeping in and completing the daily run by noon would have not been mutually exclusive, but my planned run that day was 210 minutes and I had my heart set on running some trails about 30 minutes from our house!

At first I pouted a bit and said I would "martyr" my plans (apologies to all the true martyrs in Heaven looking down and laughing—I hope—at me for that), but then I realized my wife shouldn't have to miss her party because of my running addiction. My plan: sleep in. God's plan: get going. So I got up at 5am and got going. Here is a list of the blessings I received which would not have happened had I not accepted God's plan but had, instead, spent Sunday morning sleeping in:

- Spent 30 minutes in the car, listening to great Christmas music and counting my blessings as I did my daily prayers.
- Saw two deer running through the woods and marveled at God's creation that makes running through the woods look so graceful and easy. Deer must look at us and think: "What was God thinking letting

humans dream that they can actually run out here where we rule?"

- After hearing a Zach Brown song about his father, told my Dad (who has been with Jesus, I pray, for almost 20 years now) that I missed him and I really hoped he was proud of me.
- Enjoyed a really cool view of Atlanta from close to the top of Kennesaw Mountain through the wind and light snow falling!
- Thanked God for the fact that I was able to run this trail and that I had a warm car and warm, clean clothes to change into when I was done. Prayed for all homeless people in the world, especially those in Atlanta that I met the other night when I spent the night at a homeless shelter.
- Relished the feeling of the heater in my car and changing into warm sweats and a dry shirt; would not have appreciated it so much without that cold morning run.
- Enjoyed the best sandwich I have ever tasted (due to hunger and cold, I am sure) after and thanked the Lord I could afford to purchase such a wonderful luxury.
- Spent two quality hours with my daughter, feeling so accomplished and relaxed.

Embracing R & R

Sure, I know all about the physiology and psychology of how exercise works (stimulus, micro damage, rest, repair, adaptation, and then do it all again), but that doesn't mean I have to apply it to myself, does it?

Making myself take time off from running to rest and repair is like a golfer dropping his golf clubs off for cleaning and maintenance in the middle of a tour. That's what a few days off feels to me. Not only does exercise make me feel good, but it also makes me a better boss (I think), husband (I know), father (I know), and overall person. When I don't exercise, I suck at all four!

This is where it was a really, really good idea for me to hire a coach! Most people hire coaches and trainers for motivation and program design, but I hired my coach (Matt "R", the guy who got me through Pine Mountain in under 9 hours) specifically to make me take recovery breaks and taper correctly for my races. He also helps me tweak my training plans.

So, after the Sunday morning Kennesaw Mountain run and about 10 hours running throughout the week, I made myself take a recovery week. Coach has me doing a recovery week every three weeks during this lead up to the 50 mile ultra off-road. I have to admit that I really don't hate it as much as I used to. I am training so much I really need it, and I still get to train daily, but do shorter distance at lower intensity.

CHAPTER 13

LETTING GO

Fight the good fight of the faith. Take hold of the eternal life to which you were called when you made your good confession in the presence of many witnesses.

1 Timothy 6:12

Training the will

I had been learning to rely on intense exercise, such as long trail runs, to help me clear my mind, pray, and listen for God's response. You might say that, along with the physical training I made myself do to meet the increasingly demanding challenges of the longer races over rougher terrain, I was undergoing a different kind of training at the same time. Is it possible to say that you are training your spirit or soul or will? I don't know what to call it, but I was doing interior discipline at the same time that I was doing physical discipline.

Turned out this other kind of training would come in handy when the struggles in our marriage intensified. My wife and I were married on January 15, 2000. We had dated on and off for seven years before that (we met in 1992 and were friends for almost nine months before we even went on a date or kissed). As marriages go and in line with what I "signed up for," I thought we had a wonderful and supportive marriage. Not perfect by any means, but compared to most, I was very happy and content and assumed my wife was also.

For three years at this point I had been trying everything in my power to improve the marriage, for the children's sake, if nothing else. I really thought I knew what love was when I got married, but that changed when we had kids. I literally would die for them, and maybe I will have to die a little to make this marriage better. I always felt the relationship between husband and wife came first, and if that was not good then the children would have to step back and deal with less attention until the marriage got better or split up. Now I am not so sure.

That's how things stood when, *on my long weekend run,* I realized that maybe she really was doing her best, so I just have to let go. The run allowed me to get to a place of accepting that she, and I, may not ever change and nothing I do or say will help that process – and that is OK! I will continue to pray for us, do my best as a father and husband, and realize that it could be a lot, lot worse!

One week later I was feeling completely at peace in my marriage, even though really nothing had changed, except for my attitude and perception of the situation. Which, of course, is all you can ever really change. We all know this but it's still such a surprise to see it happening (smile).

Christmas gift

Since being married, Christmas time has been a challenge, to say the least, due to the differences my wife and I have in the amount of money that should be spent on gifts. This year I did my best to "let go" and just enjoy the moment for the sake of our kids (and, quite frankly, my sanity) but it did get very rough at one point a few days before Christmas day.

I had been going back and forth daily, struggling with thoughts of our marriage and how tough it had been lately. All these thoughts were swirling in my mind, so I had to go for a run to get some peace and quiet.

Out on the trail, almost everything was covered with snow, and it was so cold you could see your breath and the only thing not snow covered was the trail itself. After 2.5 hours, my mind started to clear and I decided I would just concentrate on setting a good example myself and taking care of my family the best I could, and let my wife alone to find her own way. She might not be able to fill my need for friendship the way I would like, so I would spend more time cultivating friendships and interests outside my marriage (especially in the ultra-running community and our church).

After coming to that decision, I felt so much better that week. I was much more focused on my prayer life, physical life, and career—and family time was just amazing.

Letting go, again

We had been invited to a family New Year's Eve party, but I had been planning on a long run the next day and did not want to be hung over, so I said I would go but would not drink and would leave early. I kept a drink in hand and mingled and really had a lot of fun! No one really takes notes on what others are doing at these things, as much as my ego would like me to think they do.

After midnight I could tell my wife was having a lot of fun and so were the kids, so I said I would head home and our friend could take them home in when the party was over. I said my goodbyes and headed out the door. I have to admit, it was a depressing ride home. Earlier that week we had gone to see a movie, "Country Strong," which affected us both emotionally. On the way out of the movie she had said, "At least we still share this, getting emotional at sappy movies."

I really felt for (and identified with) the main character in this movie, troubled but trying to do the best she could. Anyway, the next morning I played the soundtrack on my iPod on the way to the trail and ended up crying the whole ride. I thought of what it would be like to be alone (like I had been the night before) and how sad that would be.

During my run I thought (again!) that it was really time to "let go" and "let God." This trying to hold on and change things was just making me so crazy. Just to confirm that message, about an hour into the run I was thinking how I was holding on too tight, and I lost concentration and tripped.

At this point I really should have just let myself fall, but instead I fought the fall and in the process really hurt my right hamstring. OK, God, I get the message—let go, relax, and stop trying to control everything!

By the end of the run I felt much better and my wife and I ended up having a really good heart to heart. This letting go business really works. I will try to let go more on a daily basis! As always, thanks to the Lord for the strong message that I certainly would not have gotten or received without the run and the music.

"Snow Jam 2011"

In 2011, the year began with a monster (for Atlanta) snowstorm and we were "stranded" (in Atlanta no one drives in snow, partly because the metro area lacks the equipment to clear the roads quickly). I found out that running is not the only way for me to quiet my mind. During those snow days, with my wife out of town and just the kids and I at home, there was plenty of time to reflect on "my road with the Lord" so far and here's what came up:

My relationship and trust in the Lord had come a long way. Used to be, when things didn't go the way I had planned at work, I would be very upset. This time, stuck at home unable to work, I found I wasn't upset about losing business. I figured it was happening for a reason and tried my best to enjoy the "forced, unpaid vacation" with my kids. Plus, with internet access I was "forced to" catch up on a lot of year end accounting projects I had been putting off!

I really, really enjoyed my time with my kids! On both days they walked two hours with Dad to the store and back as an "adventure." We had such a blast!

Sometimes I forget how much my wife does around the house when I am working (are you reading this, honey?). Between cooking, cleaning, laundry and then trying to stay caught up on rescheduling people, emails, projects, I was "snowed under" those couple of days she was gone.

Heather's workout

> At this point in the book you probably need a break and what better thing to do in your break than work out???

Have I mentioned that my wife not only runs the household—she also runs exercise groups for our business? Here's a fun workout she came up with during the "Snow Jam"… Use a deck of cards to dictate your workout. No two workouts are the same. Here's how it works:

The suit tells you what exercise to do:

    heart = mountain climber
    diamond = jumping lunge
    club = pushup
    spade = step up

The number tells you how many reps to do, with face cards as follows:

> Jacks = 11 reps
> Queens = 12 reps
> Kings = 13 reps
> Joker = 10 burpees!!

Examples:

> If you pull a 3 of spades, you do 3 step ups per leg (use a chair)
> If you pull a queen of hearts, you do 12 mountain climbers per leg
> If you pull a 6 of diamonds, you do 6 jumping lunges per leg

If you pull 2 or 3 of the same suit in a row... add them together!!

Seeing God in action with others

One of my resolutions for 2011 was to reach out more to the ultra-running community to develop new friendships with people who share an interest in this intense sport with me, and also to have company on the very long runs. I *love* training alone for a lot of reasons but when the runs get over three hours, it really, really helps to have someone with you!

I was planning a 270 minute run in the middle of January, right after the "monster" snowstorm, and I could find only one guy willing to meet me at 6 am on a weekday—imagine that! So, he pulled up in the parking lot at 6 and jumped out of the car, ready to go, but his keys stayed in. Trying to help, I suggested AAA, but he just answered with, "I'll just break the fu##kin window when we get back."

"Arrrgg," I thought, "Why did I ruin my peaceful, introspective time with the Lord like this?" But I decided to go with it anyway and see what lesson I could learn on the waySure enough, the run began with lots of angry energy and banter coming from him. A lot of his anger had to do with a mutual friend of ours, so I could tell this was going to put me in a rough place. I really did not want to take sides (there is his side, the other guy's side, and then the truth). Right away I could feel my type A (some friends say A+), controlling nature wanting to jump in and fix the problem by suggesting solutions and telling what I would do in the situation.

When I converted to Catholicism, I had a cross tattooed on my forearm, by my wrist so I would see it every day and it would remind me who is *really* in charge. Even so, it's easy to forget and fall back into the old modus operandi of solving everyone else's problems.

With this guy, I could tell right away he just needed to vent so, fortunately, I was able to remember who's really in charge and just listened. And ran. And asked leading questions like: "How long has it been since you have been to church?" and "Are you actively praying about this?" I can't take credit for deliberately planning to respond this way. It must have been that the interior training that had been going on lately as I ran (exterior training) was taking hold a little. And maybe the tattoo was helping, too. It was just becoming my normal response to people's problems. I was just finally realizing the only solution to any problem was to do your best and then give the rest to the Lord.

Looking back on our conversation after he had left, I realized there had been a real change in his affect, the tone of his banter, and his general view on things. As his defenses were worn down by the run, he became happier and more appreciative (and more forgiving of our friend) of his life. He started focusing on the good things in his life (this *always* happens to me on a run, no matter how long it is) instead of what was lacking. It really was amazing to watch God being allowed in, or, more accurately, the run wearing him down enough that he could *see* the beauty and blessings of God again. These blessings are, of course, always around us, but we're often too wound up in our own trivial problems to notice.

If only I could have kept him out there longer (he ended up doing 90 minutes), maybe he would have been open to going to Mass with me this weekend. Who knows—after five hours he might have converted. Just think—after a 50 mile run, he might have started discerning a vocation!

Anyway, this is the reason I wrote this book. Through running, I have found out how to quiet my turmoil and "let God in." And on that run I saw this same thing happen to someone else, so now I want to get the message out there to anyone who needs to "get quiet" that here is a way to do that.

CHAPTER 14

TRAINING FOR 50 MILER

The horse is made ready for the day of battle, but
victory rests with the LORD.

Proverbs 21:31

Seven weeks to go

When I started this off-road running stuff in February 2008,
I set a goal to do a 50k to see what it was like and to see
what my body and mind were capable of. Once completing
that, I set a goal to run a 50 miler before I turned 50! Not a
bad progression, I figured: an off-road 10k in January 2008
and a 50 miler in March, 2011. Believe it or not, as far as
ultra runners go, this was a very, very slow progression, but I
know myself and if I dive in too deeply, I typically get hurt
or, worse, burn out; I really, really enjoy the trails, so I didn't
want to lose that feeling because I did too much, too soon! I
had also read an article early on that the average "life span" of

an ultra runner was just three years! Now the 50 mile race was less than two months away.

With seven weeks to go before my first 50 mile off-road race, I was feeling very good after a 300 minute run (ultra runners and coaches commonly track minutes instead of miles to make it seem more attainable and not so crazy)!

I really wanted to get some time on the course and see what it was like. There was a 20 mile group run at Dawsonville National Forest (race site) planned for a Saturday in late January, but the run was cancelled (the forest was actually closed due to the snow). At first I was disappointed, but after hitting the trails down here (one hour south), I understood the wisdom of that decision.

Anyway, I ran at 6 am on one of the Chattahoochee River trails instead. It was very cold, very dark and very lonely and the whole trail was frozen. It must have melted the day before and then froze again—I was running through frozen footsteps for the whole time. I managed to do 90 minutes without falling on my ass, so I considered it a successful day. My coach's training regimen must have been working, since my ankles felt strong as they had ever been.

The next day, I met two buddies at Kennesaw Mountain and headed out for what I thought would be muddy (no snow cover) trails. I was wrong—it was about 75% covered with ice and snow! I ended up running just 220 minutes (disappointing), but it was still a great run—pain free and strong for the whole time. Losing some of that bodybuilder weight was paying off. Nutrition was great—peanut butter, honey, banana and Nutella sandwiches *rock*, btw—and mentally I was very focused and happy.

So, I ended up with 310 minutes for the weekend (not sure how many miles due to slow pace in snow) and a new appreciation for how well trail shoes work in tough conditions. Watching people try to climb Kennesaw Mountain in their church clothes while I ran full speed down in shorts and a t-shirt was very entertaining (wipe that smug smile off your face, Rami!). I had another planned 300 minute run coming up the next weekend and then (God willing) a group *night* run on the course on January 29.

Night running

Four weeks to go. I ended the week with a really cool and new experience, night running! I had done a lot of early morning running with a headlamp, but never a night run. As usual, I was both nervous and excited to be doing something new, with new people. As I do most of my training solo, I had to let go of control and accept that I would be training at an unfamiliar place with unfamiliar people, running at their pace and running, for the first time, at night—jumping right in to the deep end!

Anyway, we all had maps but I knew I would get hopelessly lost if I tried to go it on my own, so I vowed to run as fast or slow as I needed to stay with a group that knew where they were going. It really was a blast, since running at night takes away all the cues you use for pacing and exertion (and time elapsed) and the time went by so fast! At one point I suggested—OK, told—my group to stop and turn off our headlamps and the stars were amazing!

Before I knew it we were back and had run 13 miles. I was not tired at all and felt like I could run all night (a good thing given that, God willing, I'll be running 37 miles farther on March 5). Our group waited around a bonfire for the other runners who were running the full 20 mile loop (my coach wanted me to do only 150 minutes for my long run this week so I held myself back). Driving home I felt wonderful and very confident about this race. Except for some serious mud sections, the course was much easier than the trail I usually train on and *very* much easier than other race courses I have done.

After that, I ended up with 300 minutes for the week, with double long runs planned for the next week (210 and then 180 minutes on back-to-back days). Then I would have to "taper" for 2 weeks (tapering for trail races is much shorter than for road races as the regular training beats you up a lot less). Deliberately cutting back my training time had always been my absolute least favorite part of the training plan. I promised myself I would train so hard the next 2 weeks that I could embrace and enjoy the tapering.

I found myself once again in a place of complete appreciation and gratitude that I could even attempt this journey. The lessons learned on the trail had been absolutely life-giving. I was really looking forward to 12 hours or so of joy on March 5!

9 Days to Go!

I could not believe after 18 weeks (or 33 years, depending on how you looked at it) of training that my attempt at a 50 mile trail run was just that close! I had completed my longest training run at 5 hours (about 30 miles) and felt great so I had huge confidence after that. Then, a week later, I had attempted a three hour run (17 mile loop at Kennesaw) and felt absolutely horrible, but this ended up being a good sign! I had been training hard and now it was time to embrace the taper. Perfect timing to go to NY and visit my mom!

In NY, I had to do road running again since the trails were covered with three feet of snow. Actually, I did try running about a mile on the trails on the first day since it was 16 degrees (8 with wind chill) and the snow was frozen over, but it really didn't count as running—more like fast hiking with body sledding in between!

On my return from NY, tapering began in earnest, with a short 90 minute run on the weekend and then 30-45 minutes of either spinning or light running up until the race. I would take Thursday completely off and then run 25 minutes Friday to loosen up the legs (achy knees and very flat, dead feeling legs which always happens during my taper but never ceases to worry me). I worked a half day on Friday and tried to take in as much salty and low fiber food as possible as early as possible to sustain my body during the race.

The race would start the next day at 6:30 am and, God willing, I would be crossing the finish line around 6:30 pm.

My goals for the race were to,

1. First and foremost, connect with the Lord somewhere along the path and to:
2. Finish the race.
3. Finish the race without injury.
4. Finish the race without injury, feeling strong and smiling.
5. Finish the race without injury, feeling strong and smiling, in under 12 hours.

CHAPTER 15

THE "FINAL" CHAPTER

Join with me in suffering, like a good soldier of
Christ Jesus. No one serving as a soldier gets involved
in civilian affairs; rather, they try to please their
commanding officer. Similarly, anyone who competes
as an athlete does not receive the victor's crown except
by competing according to the rules.

2 Timothy 2:3-6

Training program summary

My coach and I had designed a "loose" 18 week training
program, flexed around my need to lose a little of that
bodybuilder bulk and learn how to rest and recover. Overall it
went really well. Here are the highlights:

Average week training: 450 minutes of running, or about
37.5–45 miles, depending on courses ran.

Total training time: 7550 minutes or about 630 miles (half the distance to NY from Atlanta)!

Body changes since December 2009:

- Lost 13 lbs. (from 210 down to 197)
- Lost 14% of total body fat (from 15% down to 12.9%)

Restrictions at two weeks before race:

- no painkillers (e.g., ibuprofen)
- no simple sugar except in training runs
- no alcohol
- plenty of sleep

Actual Training Log
Race day prep
Actual Food For Race

My wife was "standing in" for me on a Cub Scout trip to sleep over at the Tennessee Aquarium, so she and our two children left that night. They would meet me at the race about midway. I had the house to myself, which was actually pretty nice given that I am a bit crazy the day before these things. Felt very relaxed and calm after packing all my stuff in the car and settling down to rest my legs for the night. Read Dean Karnazes' new book *Run* and it put everything I was about to do in complete perspective: if he could get through what he has done with a positive attitude, tomorrow would be nothing!

I fell asleep right away at 8:45 pm and slept through the night—no nightmares of forgetting everything and not being able to run. Up at 3:30 am to the sound of light rain (fantastic!) and feeling good. Said some calm prayers to have a good day, stay in the moment, and be open to whatever God had in store for me. Downstairs right away to eat my first meal (wanted to get in most of my calories pre-race about 2-3 hours before the start): Peanut Butter, Nutella and banana sandwich on white bread (not my normal breakfast to say the least) and a cup of coffee. Hot shower to loosen up and then second breakfast, a shake:

- 2 bananas
- 1 scoop vanilla protein powder
- 2 tbs. peanut butter
- Splenda
- Ice
- Water
- 1 tbs. Chia seeds
- 1 Imodium (not in the shake!)

With about 1000 calories in me and feeling a bit sick (imagine taking all that in before 4 am) I was ready (nutritionally, that is). Feeling sick is a good sign for me as it means I took in enough and would not be tempted to "nervous eat" anymore before the start, just sip on water and low calorie electrolyte drink.

A good friend picked me up so I would not have to drive home after (this is very, very important after an Ultra, even if it is only 45 minutes)! It was nice to have someone to talk to and, as I was starting to get nervous, nice to have a distraction from thinking about the race (and how wonderful the trails would be as it was still raining and was projected to rain all day!) We left at 4:45 am for a 6:30 am start.

I normally absolutely *love* to run in the rain, and really love cold rain since it distracts me from the pain, the woods are really beautiful with rain falling, and it keeps my core temperature down which has always been an issue for me. This trail we were running on was a bit of a different story. Most trails are pretty hard packed and thus just get wet and a bit slippery when it rains. This trail is probably 75% or more soft Georgia clay and is often used for horseback riding, so it is really torn up. Translation: *The craziest, toughest running conditions I have ever, ever run in my 33 years of running!* Add to this it was my first attempt at 50 miles (btw, in very typical Ultra Running course measurement, this race ended up being 53 miles–might not sound like much of a difference but, oh, it was).

One of the things I absolutely love about this sport and the type of people it attracts is there is no room (especially on a day like this) for any negative attitude whatsoever. Those that know me know that I tend to be an eternal optimist, but even I was a bit taken aback by this course when we did the first loop—a great test of my positive attitude, I can tell you that! Just to give you an idea, people who had trained on this course 5-7 days after a rain storm reported that it was almost not runnable (or walkable), especially the hills, and we would be running it, with 200 others, all day in the rain—again, yea!!!

Got to the start and got dressed in the car as it was still a light rain, set up my little "oasis" of a chair (which I swore I wouldn't sit in until the end), food, change of shoes and socks, etc.

Funny story about how weird your mind works when you are nervous. About 10 minutes from the start, for some reason I put my water bottle down (you really need this as some aid stations are 6 miles apart and in these conditions that can take over an hour) on my chair. While in the tent listening to race instructions and talking to my friend, I forgot that I had left my water bottle at my chair. I was totally convinced someone had stolen my water bottle and was running around frantically trying to find it, even asking one of the volunteers to help me and she told the race director to announce it (just to show you how wonderful other racers are, no less than 3 people offered me an extra bottle they had). When I ran back to the chair to get my own extra bottle, there it was. So embarrassing, I couldn't even apologize or explain. Chalk it up to nervousness!

First lap

We started off in the dark and rain. The course was a 13 mile loop, back to the start/finish, then a 7 mile loop. You did both loops 2x and then one more of the 13 mile loop to total 53 miles. I had never done a loop course before and I wasn't sure if I would like it (seeing the finish line 4x before you are done) but I actually loved it! It was so nice to have something to look forward to—people, food, family—every lap and it helped break down the race into many different finish lines: i.e., I will allow myself a Red Bull and Peanut M&M's after I finish 20 miles—that kind of thing! Anyway, that first lap was a real lesson in how to run in Georgia clay mud (I kept thinking if someone video-taped us trying to get through the really deep sections and especially the steep uphills, it would look like a really long version of "America's Funniest Home Videos").

The biggest mental lesson I learned in this lap was to avoid people who were not completely positive. Luckily, as I mentioned, 99% of people who choose to do this for "fun" are overall the nicest, happiest, most positive people I have ever met, but there are a few in any crowd and given the conditions and my tendency to have some very low points in these races, I didn't want to be around anything or anyone that would bring me down. When I ran up alongside of one guy and girl who were whining about the mud, how long it would take us, and how the 7 mile loop was so much harder than the 13, I knew I had to break away from them ASAP. No judgment—I just couldn't let myself fall into that trap.

From then on, everyone I met and everyone I talked to was positive and having a *great* day! This was really the theme for the day and I was so glad for my newly found faith in the

Lord and how it has taught me an even deeper appreciation for the blessings I have in life: not just the physical gift to be able to do this but the mental strength to remain positive when things get tough. Just goes to show that ultra marathons are a perfect metaphor for life!

The first lap was tough but was done in 2 hours, 30 minutes—not bad at all considering the conditions. Now out to the dreaded 7 mile loop. The hills were tough but not as muddy as those in the 13 mile loop and, because it was only 7 miles with one aid station, it was easier to break it down into manageable segments. This breaking things down became a theme throughout the day (again, a metaphor for life): only 1 hour 'till next aid station, only 4.7 miles to start /finish, only have to do that killer hill 2 more times. Really helped, trust me! Throughout the first 20 miles I felt OK, but after 20 miles I felt fantastic.

I had been anticipating the low that I usually get after 3-4 hours, but it never came. I had told more people about this race than ever before and had asked everyone to pray for me to stay positive and upbeat, especially during the low times. This did two things for me: first of all, I had made myself accountable to many people to not drop out when things got tough (which helped). More importantly, however, I really felt the prayers helped me stay happy and motivated during the toughest conditions I had ever raced in!

Round two

The next 13 miles were actually better than the first as it finally stopped raining for about 3 hours and I knew I would be seeing my family on the next loop through. At this point I had adopted a strange way to climb the muddy hills, sort of a "duck walk" like I was going uphill on skis. Without this "duck walk," I would have fallen back down the hill or gotten stuck wondering where to put my foot down next (real "America's Funniest Video" stuff!).

At this point, I started getting a little over-confident and picked up my pace on the down hills and was chatting with a nice guy while we rounded an easy corner and BAM, my first fall of the day. Must have sounded bad cause the another guy in front of me yelled, "Oh sh#t, are you ok?" I was fine, just a little dirty and banged up, glad to have the first fall out of the way. I almost fell again after about a half mile and wrenched my knee in the process. Then I fell going up a hill (very slow) and caught myself (going even slower) falling up another hill. Two falls and one near miss in under 1 mile (more funny video footage).

I really cannot explain how crazy this mud was: hundreds of footprints filled with water, the whole trail covered with shoe-sucking mud and water, which slowed us down to a shuffle (walking is even worse than running because you sink farther down). Definitely was a new, exciting and fun experience that I need do only once in my life to feel satisfied. My feet and legs were so muddy and so caked (they would get muddy, dry over and then get muddy again) that my wife said they looked like "elephant legs." You couldn't even tell I had shoes and socks on! We just kept running straight down the "orange river," as we started calling it. I never knew how deep the river was; couldn't tell if my shoe might get stuck in the river mud or, worse, were about to get stuck in the thicker mud off to the side and pull my foot out from under me.

At the end of 33 miles, I finally saw my family, real quick, as I didn't want to linger too long at the loop start-again point. I had learned in these things to keep forward momentum going as much as possible: I couldn't let myself even think about the finish (or in this case, dry clothes, warm food, and a clean warm house) until I was about an hour out. I told them I would see them in a couple hours.

This loop was uneventful except I fell one more time and let go of thinking about time goals. Given the conditions, I really wanted to make it and not be stressing about getting in under some arbitrary number (i.e., 12 hours), so I just let go. I even took my watch off so I wouldn't look at it anymore! Maybe that's why—even with the poor conditions—my marathon, 50k, and 40 mile time splits in this race were faster than they had been the previous times I had run just those distances. Obviously I am lighter and in much better shape and I will tell you I allowed myself to entertain what "would have been" if the course had been dry, and actually 50 miles, but not for long; pretty quickly I got back to enjoying the day for what it was.

Final loop

Now I could smell the finish. One more 13 mile loop to go. Our progress was so slow—my family was able to drive home, take naps, and still get back for the finish! At that point, the heavens opened up and it poured, I mean really rained, for the next three hours straight. At least it wasn't too cold—at this point I was running in just shorts and a dry fit t-shirt. I actually felt really strong at this point. Even after nine hours of mud-slogging I still could run the down hills and some flats and was enjoying the rain.

My ipod just wasn't liking the rain, so, I had to be content with the sound of my breathing, the sloshing of my feet, and the sound of the rain, tough at first but meditative after a while.

This was now my third loop on the 13 miles so I had some idea of what I was in for, although the mind (another wonderful God-design here) has a neat way of eliminating your short term memory in these things: I kept forgetting about the killer, muddy hill I would be soon facing again! I would tell myself to do certain things on "the next uphill," such as take off or put on a jacket, drink water, eat, take salt pills; at one point I was walking uphill for at least five minutes trying to remember what I had said I would do and then I remembered—I had to pee like crazy!

With about four miles to go, a young kid (probably about 23) asked if he could run with me (after 26.2 miles we all like company) and I said sure. Turns out he was signed up for the

100 miler and was dropping out. We ran together for a while but I was feeling really strong and was getting numb and it was getting dark and I didn't have my headlamp and he was running so slow I couldn't stay back with him, but it was only a half mile from the finish so I am sure he made it OK. I ran great from there, walked a bit, and then saw the fence that marked the 100 yards-to-go point.

The finish was actually anti-climactic: it was pouring, dark, and cold, so most of the spectators and crews were under shelter. It was really strange to have trained this long and run for this long under such tough conditions and have no one at the finish to greet me (my family was late getting back). But I had been trying to accept whatever comes my way in my life as God's plan, so I didn't give in to that feeling. In a way, it was kind of appropriate, however, as most of my training had been done alone, for most of my race I had been alone, and I was doing this to get closer to the Lord, which I do best alone.

And, too, there were three races going on at once, so no one knew if you were finishing the 50k or 50m or heading out for another lap for the 100m. There was just one guy there who said, "We've got a finisher here," and a couple of little kids clapped. So different from the Ironman race and so appropriate.

I headed for the food tent and grabbed some hot pizza and a soda and finally sat down after 12 solid hours of trail running! I realized the huge "down" I had been waiting for in the race had never showed up. Emotionally, this was the most even-keeled I had ever been in one of these events (result of training? prayers? both?). My wife and kids, however, did show up with dry clothes and cold beer, and we sat and chatted for a bit. We were all exhausted so we didn't stay around long, in spite of my original plan to camp out that night and watch everyone finish. I felt really good about my accomplishment and thanked the Lord for bringing me home safely.

Race exertion: 53 miles in 12 hours—10,000 calories burned

Race nutrition (about 300 calories per hour):

- 1 bottle water and 2 e-caps (salt) every hour
- 5 gels total
- peanut butter and honey/Nutella and banana sandwiches
- pretzels, bananas, peanut m & m's, fig newtons
- 3 regular Red Bulls at 20, 33, and 40 miles
- one potato with salt
- 2 cups chicken soup with Ramen noodles

When results were posted on Monday, I looked at the 100 mile results first (only 17 finished out of 56 starters, only 4 under 24 hours) and then took a break and told myself I would hold on to my good feeling of accomplishment no matter what my results were. Amazingly, I was 12th overall out of 73 finishers (not sure how many signed up or started, maybe about 100) and first in the 45-49 age group! Just goes to show you: this is a good sport for my strengths: I am too big to put on great speed and really don't have natural athletic ability, *but* I've got tons of determination and stubborn, never-say-die, stick-to-it-iveness! The power of perseverance!

Recovery went well: I was still very sore and tired on Monday but felt recovered enough to do a 30 minute easy spin and stretch a bit. Had a beer to relax those tight muscles! My big, determined body held up incredibly well. My longest training run was only five hours and I was able to run 12 hours almost continuously!

Lessons from the journey

- Hats off to the brave souls who attempted the 100 miler and the 17 even braver souls who ran through the rainy, cold night and finished before the 30 hour cut-off.
- I may have been tired, muddy and cold, but I had a warm shower and bed to return to that night, whereas men and women in our armed forces do this for days on end, in harm's way, sleeping on the ground in tents (if they are lucky). I tried to think of them, pray for them, and give thanks to the Lord that I am so blessed every chance I could during the 12 hours I was out there!
- Prayer works, period.
- Other people praying for you works even better, period.
- Training alone is fun, but racing alone is not.
- Running without music is ok—you really get into a rhythm and flow.
- The people who volunteer at these things are my heroes, so I want to give back and volunteer at one this year!

- I really need to get more involved in the ultra community if I want to do more of these, just to be around people who I don't have to explain myself to!
- The longer you exercise, especially if you achieve a meditative state, the simpler your mind becomes.
- Giving my best effort and learning something about myself matters much more than finishing with a strong time.
- As much as I hate it, tapering works, period.
- I need to surround myself with positive people.
- We are all capable, with faith in the Lord, of doing so much more than we think we can. Trust me on this.
- Pizza and mint chocolate chip ice cream are evidence of God's eternal love for us and even better after running 53 miles!

CHAPTER 16

WHAT'S NEXT?

Victory comes from you, O Lord. May you bless your people.

Psalm 3:8 (NLT)

100 miles?

After my 53 mile race, with no concrete goal to work toward after that, training became apathetic and just not really fun. Lots of people can train "just to be in shape," but I am definitely not one of them! So, what to do, what to do? Ever since I had done my first trail race back in 2008 and heard that those crazy people who actually could run for 100 miles straight, it had been in the back of my mind…now it moved to the front of my mind! I approached this decision, however, with much more thought, prayer, and discussion with the whole family than I had for any previous event.

I even met with a good friend and very experienced ultra runner to get his ideas on how to approach this. I did not talk to him about training or racing, but, instead, about how he works his training schedule around his obligations as business owner, husband, and dad. And, I wanted to know how he stayed grounded in his faith.

Making this demanding sport work within my life so it enhances, rather than disrupts, my relationship with my family and the Lord would be better than the end goal of finishing 100 miles itself! He talked me out of picking an "easy" 100 miler and reminded me why I had gotten into this sport in the first place: to get closer to the Lord by testing myself physically and mentally and to retrieve that sense of fear and adventure that I, like so many people in our planned, protected and distracted society, really need!

I talked it over some more with other friends, had my coach draw up a training plan to maintain fitness year round and then do mega mileage training 4-6 weeks before the race. Once I looked at the plan and started to work the training into my regular weekly schedule, it started to become more real. Finally, I signed up for the Pinhoti 100, a point-to-point (no looping) 100 mile trail run in Alabama coming up seven months later (it was late April when I signed up) on November 5-6.

The minute I signed up I felt better. More focused, excited, definitely scared (but in a great way) and more *alive*! This is a really big undertaking to say the least. Not just the training, but the logistics. I had realized how important it is when running a long race to recruit a crew, pacers, support people, training partners, massage therapists, drug dealers (kidding), and so on. What a great lesson and metaphor for life—we cannot do this alone!

So, I started seeking out others to train with and, more importantly, pace and crew me through the night. Yes, we start at 6 am Saturday and the cut-off is noon Sunday! Most people who finish (a very high percent drop out) are on the trail between 24-30 hours...over a day on your feet! One of the popular blogs on this type of race offers this suggestion to get a feel for how exhausted you might feel during the race: Work a full day on Friday, no nap, have dinner with your family and say good-night, and then run through the night until Saturday morning! It really sounds like an awesome adventure to me and I thank the Lord daily that he has given me the gift to even attempt this; if I have what it takes to finish remains to be seen in seven months.

Running with others

I really, really like to do new things! I also like to do things that get me "outside of my box" and scare me a bit. Two of my new training companions are training for their first ultra this summer: the Lake Tahoe 50 miler. They are both fairly accomplished distance runners, but neither have ever done an off-road trail ultra and Tahoe is very, very hard: minimum elevation is about 6500 feet and maximum is close to 10,000 feet. These are my kind of guys!

They invited me to a training run on the Appalachian Trail. Four hours of super hilly mountain running would be a good start up for my 100 mile training. When they started running about 50 yards in, on a hill that was about 20% grade, I decided to keep with them, even though I was pretty sure it would hurt me later. They were in much better shape than me, since I hadn't done any long runs since the 50 miler and they were doing back-to-back runs every weekend. "It's going to be a long, lonely day," I caught myself thinking.

But it wasn't. The trail was challenging, all right: serious climbs followed by beautiful ridges and downhill sections, surrounded by ferns and spreading shade trees the whole way. We "ran" to the top of Springer Mountain which is the official start of the Appalachian Trail (the 6.5 miles is considered the "approach trail") and back in about 4 hours.

I have noticed that when I run with others, especially those in good enough shape to talk the whole time, I do not have as many, if any, "connection to God" moments as I do when I train solo. Most of my revelations come after the run, when I have cleared my mind and am peaceful enough to absorb the messages and lessons God wants to show me that day. Running with others has its place in my training for sure, especially on days when I need "safety in numbers." I have come to enjoy both equally, but as far as "quieting the noise" and hearing God during the run, nothing beats the quiet time of running solo, especially early in the morning.

Avoidance

I found myself in "maintenance mode" for the next two months until real training for the 100 miler began in earnest. Even maintenance, however, can be pretty intense compared to an average runner's program. My weekly totals typically ranged between 300-500 minutes (30-50 miles on the trails) and my long runs had been ranging from a quick 120 minutes before an early baseball game to 240 minutes of really, really fun and challenging running/hiking on the Appalachian Trail.

It's a big surprise to friends, training clients, and training partners that getting up to run or workout is *not* always easy for me. Most people I coach will invariably throw back at me (usually when I am giving them a tough time for missing a workout) that "this is easy for you—you love getting up before dawn to work out." I get up most days of the week at 4:30 am and either run, do recovery cardio, or lift weights with a club member/training client. Every day, and I mean every day, I hit the snooze (at least once) and have a short conversation with myself about getting up. Usually it goes like this:

"Wow, I am tired. I wonder if I can get one of my team members to cover my training session".

"Nope, can't do that, it would be irresponsible and I would lose income that my family needs."

"Let me just hit the snooze one more time".

"*Get Up!*"

"Ok, I am up, thanking the Lord for giving me the ability and a reason to get up so early and for letting me be the best version of myself today. 'Lord, let me be open to the path that you put forth for me today.' See? I'm up!"

Perfect example:. I had gone out on a very nice "date" with my wife the previous night. We had gone to a movie place that serves food and alcohol. My wife was driving so I decided to have a few drinks (without eating much dinner— bad move!). Didn't get to sleep until midnight and the alarm went off at 4:30 am for a 5:15 am training session at the club. My first thought was, "Wow, I am tired and a bit hung over and dehydrated—I feel like I just fell asleep 4.5 hours ago". My conversation went on like this: "You *know* for a fact that if you get up, train your client, and then go for a run you will feel physically great, have a productive and peaceful day and, most importantly, do the things that God put you on this earth to do. So get your ass up!"

I decided to apply my own advice to myself. I told myself I would just go out for 30 minutes, something "easy to accomplish," with no high expectations for the workout. Also, I reminded myself how great it would feel, both physically and psychologically, even if I only completed a small percent of my planned workout (instead of blowing it off). So, I headed out the door with enough food and water (and some cash in case a miracle happened and I stayed out longer than planned) to run long but with the "permission" to cut it short if my body did not respond well to the warm up portion of the run.

Guess what? Twenty minutes into the run I was in a great mood and my body felt great (this happens about 90% of the time if I just force myself to go out for a "little bit"). I ended up going three hours (I won't lie, the last 30 minutes were really tough due to the dehydration) and about 17 miles and I felt awesome the rest of the day!

One of those lessons I have to "learn" over and over— sometimes the Nike AD really is right. Don't think about it too much. "Just Do It."

Change of plans

Plans changed, as they often do. As I mentioned when I talked about signing up for my first 100 mile trail run, I did it because it felt like the timing was right. My training was progressing well, the 50 (53) miler had gone well, I was injury free (aches and pains are just a part of our sport so I don't count those) and our business had started to pick up again, so I had the time and support at work to train more. Then some major things changed at work and I had to take back some roles I had delegated to others.

At first I was upset and disappointed, but then, I accepted that God had a plan for me, my business, my family, and my hobbies, and I needed to accept and follow whatever changes he lays before me. Trust in him and all would be fine. I decided it was a sign that this is just not the year to do a "hundo" and emailed the race director to postpone my entry to 2012. I would still be running the Mystery Mountain marathon (the hardest trail marathon I had ever done – remember, the one I mentioned I would *never* do again!) in October and would train very hard for this race as it had absolutely kicked my butt the past two times I had done it—this year I would kick its butt!

After making that decision, I had about a day of sadness and lack of direction and then I hit the ground running, so to speak. I recommitted to work and saw some really good results there and, amazingly, was still been able to squeeze in some very cool and fun training runs, including a five hour "jaunt" on the AT. If things get more settled down, I planned to find an ultra for the spring of 2012 because I love training in the winter, but meanwhile, I'm just going to take it one day at a time.

Also, I was really looking forward to the next weekend—I would be running my first "real" race (he had done a couple of fun runs in the past) with my 9 year old son! It was a 4 mile race which ended at home plate in Turner Field: Father's Day 4 Miler!

4 miles of bliss

I have always been careful about not pushing my interests in sports on my kids. I don't want them feel to like they were forced to do something just because I love it. Kids who are forced into participation often end up having bad memories. Once my son started getting a lot of positive comments from his baseball coaches on how fast he could run and how effortless it looked when he ran laps, the moment was right! When I asked him if he was interested in doing a race, he jumped on it. We settled on the "Father's Day Four Miler" at

Turner Field; registration included tickets to the Braves' game. Watching him progress during two months of training from a 1.5 run/walk to his 41 minute four miler was so satisfying!

It was such a blessing to see him jump out of bed at 6 am saying he was "so excited and nervous I couldn't sleep" and later to see the huge smile on his face when he saw 2000 other people lining up to race with him! God was with us and gave us a cool, overcast morning and he gave us both peace in our hearts to be in the moment the whole time together. I was so focused on making sure he was OK and doing well, I had no time to think about myself, work, my marriage—nothing but the moment. I suppose God gave me that ability to be in the moment even when running with someone else because it was with someone I love more than life itself! I am so proud of how my boy ran with heart and joy, sprinting the end to beat his dad, and ended up being the fastest nine-year-old in the whole race!

I had never really had any expectations that Ryan or Hana would "follow in my footsteps" and I really still don't. It was just such a gift from God to be able to spend time with him training and doing an actual competition (during our training runs we had often ended up doing more hiking and looking for bugs and turtles than running). It was just a good day all around and the start of an amazing Father's Day weekend! Another example that the things in life that really matter are not material and don't cost a whole lot!

EPILOGUE

RUNNING AND FORGIVENESS

Wednesday nights are typically "date night" for my wife and me. They don't always turn out the way we had intended. On a recent date night, we started fighting about five minutes into the drive and it escalated to the point that we never made it to the actual date—just sat in the car for two hours arguing. We had reached a truce by the time we got home, but it was far from over.

The next morning I had a long run planned before I left for NY to clean out my mother's house. About an hour into the run I started mentally composing a long email to my wife, going over what I meant by the things that I said and what the underlying feelings were. Then I thought about what an email like that would do. It might make me feel more "right," but would it bring us closer together? I revised the email into an apology for the mean things I had said in the heat of the moment and proposed that we just move on.

In order to have time to get the email down on paper while everything was fresh in my mind, I had to end my run early (but it was worth it!). The email focused on the good things that had come out of the night's conversation (much easier to see with a clear mind) and hoped we could just move on and learn our lessons from what happened. At this same time, my wife was in a Bible study coming to very similar conclusions. When she read my email she was crying and laughing at the same time and agreed with me 100%.

So, in 24 hours, we went from a *huge* fight back to a peaceful, forgiving, and understanding couple. Could I have done this without this run? Maybe, but I guarantee it would not have happened the next day. Maybe the next week, or month, or year and not so well.

Again, running is not the only way to find God and listen to his messages—it just happens to work for me. However I feel we *all* need a vehicle that allows us to find a quiet place, away from distractions, to reflect and have enough time to process.

TO WRAP IT UP...

It's been said that our God accommodates our human limitations by making himself available to us in a way we can receive him. Certainly that is at least part of what the Incarnation is about. And that is what this story has been about—I hope. It's my story about how God connected with me through my passion for intense sports. I keep saying that I found God, but just maybe God found me, too, as I hope he will find you.

APPENDIX

SETTING GOALS

I would like to shed some light based on my personal experience in achieving athletic goals and, more importantly, seeing clients achieve goals over the past 20+ years of personal fitness training. Among the clients we work with in our business, the most common reasons for failing to achieve goals are:

Poorly defined goals

The first time I meet a client, I try to take time to help them clearly define and quantify their fitness goals. For instance, most clients say they want to "lose weight". The most important goal in changing body shape/composition is to lose body fat and maintain or increase your muscle, so the first thing I try to do is to explain the difference between getting "lean" and seeing the scale move downward. Most of the time, we try to change this goal to losing body fat, and then assigning a number to how much they want to lose per month (say 1%).

Unrealistic goals

Setting goals too high is a very common mistake which even "veterans" make at times. It is the trainer's job to make sure goals are realistic and attainable. Most of the time this means lowering expectations or breaking down long-term goals (say losing 25% of body fat, lowering cholesterol 30 points or increasing hamstring mobility by 50%) into attainable, short term goals.

Failure to accept limitations

Some people will spend their life trying to attain a body type/ leanness that only 2-3% of the population can ever attain. That 2-3% just has the right genes, plain and simple. This is not to say that all of us cannot change the way we look ("Choice, not chance, determines your destiny"), but trying to have a body that is only attainable by severe, life-long deprivation and hours of daily exercise is a sure recipe for life-long frustration! Which leads me to the next, and most common obstacle to achieving your fitness goals…

Lack of commitment

This is, without a doubt, the biggest problem I see in attaining goals. Almost everyone that comes through our door wants to look good, feel good, and be healthy. Almost everyone also does not understand, or accept, the amount of commitment it takes to achieve the goals they share with us the first day they come in. We have to work on matching these!

Before beginning an exercise program, take time to weigh what you are willing to sacrifice in order to achieve the goals you are shooting for. Remember all along your "journey", that "life happens" and allow yourself the latitude to change those goals (either more conservative or more aggressive) based upon what is happening in your life. I measure "success" as finding a program that will make you feel happy and accomplished for a lifetime. To succeed, I have found it helps to:

1. Write down, and constantly re-evaluate, both short and long term goals.
2. Ensure that goals are realistic and attainable based on current circumstances.
3. Accept necessary sacrifices and changes and be willing to work as hard as it takes to achieve goals.

And, don't forget to.... Praise God!

Made in the USA
Columbia, SC
15 September 2017